MIND OVER MOMENT

Transform Overthinking into Mindful Living for Lasting Peace

Published by: Amelie Brooks

Amelie Brooks

Copyright 2024 All rights reserved.

No part of this publication may be copied, reproduced in any format, by any means, electronic or otherwise, without prior consent from the copyright owner and publisher of this book.

Disclaimer

This book is intended to provide helpful information and strategies for managing stress, overthinking, and improving overall well-being. It is not a substitute for professional advice, diagnosis, or treatment. If you are experiencing significant emotional distress, anxiety, depression, or other mental health concerns, we strongly recommend seeking guidance from a licensed mental health professional, therapist, or medical practitioner. The content of this book is meant to complement - not replace - professional care and should be used as a tool to support your journey toward well-being. Results may vary, and it's crucial to approach personal growth with patience and an open mind.

Table of Contents:

Introduction 4

Practical Realization 7

Chapter 1: Understanding the Overthinking Phenomenon 10

Chapter 2: Discovering Mindfulness: From Ancient Wisdom to Modern Practice 26

Chapter 3: Mindful Breathing Techniques 39

Chapter 4: Healing Through Meditation: Breaking Free from Overthinking 54

Chapter 5: Emotion Regulation through Mindfulness 68

Chapter 6: Body Scan Meditation: Bridging Mind and Body ... 83

Chapter 7: Mindful Movement and Activity 98

Chapter 8: Building Sustainable Mindfulness Habits 113

Chapter 9: Real-Life Applications and Benefits 125

Chapter 10: The Path to Inner Peace 141

How This Book Helped Megan on Her Journey to Get Better 156

Conclusion 159

Reader Acknowledgement 163

References 164

Amelie Brooks

Introduction

Imagine: It's 2 AM, and you're lying in bed, your mind racing with thoughts about work deadlines, family commitments, and unresolved issues of the day. Each worry spirals into the next, trapping you in an endless loop of anxiety. As you stare at the ceiling, hoping for sleep, a series of "what-ifs" flood your consciousness. What if you don't meet that deadline? What if you forgot something noteworthy at work? An inner voice insists that rest will remain elusive unless you solve these problems now, yet the more you focus, the more problematic sleep becomes. Sound familiar?

Overthinking is a common experience in our fast-paced, hyperconnected world. The constant influx of information overwhelms even the healthiest minds, leading to stress and analysis paralysis. We find ourselves second-guessing every decision, replaying conversations in our heads, and often losing sight of the present moment. It's a pervasive challenge that affects our mental health and overall quality of life. Knowing this, the urgency of addressing overthinking becomes clear.

What if there were a way to interrupt this cycle and reclaim peace of mind? Enter mindfulness. A powerful antidote to overthinking. Imagine replacing restless mental chatter with a soothing awareness, where each breath is a tool for calm and every moment an opportunity to reconnect with yourself. Mindfulness isn't just a buzzword; it's a practical approach proven to help break free from the chains of overthinking. Mindfulness clears mental clutter by focusing on the present moment without judgment, fostering clarity and peace.

This book offers you a pathway to begin this transformative journey. As you turn these pages, you'll discover actionable tools to combat overthinking, from simple breathing techniques to enriching meditation practices. Each chapter is designed to guide you gently and effectively toward greater peace and presence in your daily life. Whether standing in line at the coffee shop or facing a difficult decision at work, these techniques can be applied anywhere, offering moments of relief and insight when needed.

The importance of emotional intelligence cannot be overstated, especially when navigating life's stressors. Developing emotional intelligence through mindfulness equips you with enhanced self-awareness, empathy, and resilience. Understanding your emotions might change how you interact with others, allowing for more meaningful connections and less reactivity in tense situations. Mindfulness is critical in building this intelligent approach to emotions, transforming how you engage with the world.

For those seeking personal growth, mindfulness offers a toolkit to enhance your journey. By cultivating presence and patience, you'll find yourself better able to cope with challenges across different aspects of life. Staying grounded amid chaos can make all the difference in relationships, career pursuits, or personal aspirations. This book provides a roadmap for integrating mindfulness into your daily routine, empowering you to live with intention and authenticity.

As you dive deeper into reading, expect to explore a wide range of topics and techniques tailored to nurture your mental well-being. From learning to embrace silence and solitude to harnessing the power of intentional breathing, you'll gain the confidence to practice mindfulness regardless of your surroundings. Despite the external chaos, internal calm becomes attainable through consistent practice and dedication.

Yet it's crucial to set realistic expectations for this journey; mindfulness takes time and patience to internalize. It won't eliminate stress but will fundamentally change your relationship with it. Instead of being consumed by anxious thoughts, you'll learn to observe them, understand their origins, and reduce their impact. Readers are encouraged to approach this book with openness and curiosity, ready to experiment and adapt strategies that best suit their lifestyles.

In essence, mindfulness is about companionship with oneself. A process of getting to know who you are beneath the layers of habitual thought patterns and societal conditioning. It's an invitation to rediscover joy in simplicity and acknowledge the abundant beauty in moments often overlooked. When fully embraced, mindfulness extends beyond a personal tool. It becomes a way of life.

Let's embark on this journey together, exploring how mindfulness can reshape your experiences, bring balance, and restore peace of mind. Each step forward in this practice is not just progress but a celebration of newfound perspectives and capabilities. Within these pages lies the promise of transformation, guiding you on an ongoing quest for calm and clarity amidst a chaotic world. Welcome the opportunity to transform overthinking into mindful living. Where each moment becomes a gateway to a fuller, more prosperous existence.

Practical Realization

This book primarily focuses on the theoretical aspects of managing overthinking and cultivating mindfulness. However, I recognize that theory alone can sometimes feel abstract or challenging to apply. To bridge this gap, I introduce a fictional character, Megan, who will help bring these strategies to life. At the end of each chapter, Megan will share how she applies the tips and techniques discussed to her own experiences, making them more relatable and practical for you.

Megan serves as a guide, demonstrating how theoretical concepts can be translated into everyday actions. While she may not represent every individual's unique situation, her journey reflects common challenges and aspirations for better mental well-being. Rather than focusing on her specific circumstances, Megan embodies a commitment to making these strategies tangible and emphasizes the importance of flexible, mindful approaches over rigid solutions.

Through Megan's experiences, you'll see that managing to overthink and fostering emotional resilience doesn't require a perfect formula. It's about adaptable, thoughtful practices that support a fulfilling, balanced life.

Amelie Brooks

Here is the profile of Megan:

Character Sheet: Megan Harper

- **Name**: Megan Harper
- **Age**: 27
- **Gender**: Female
- **Relationship Status**: Single
- **Family Situation**: Estranged from her father; close with her mother and younger brother
- **Average Income**: $45,000 per year
- **Professional Background**: Marketing Coordinator at a mid-sized tech firm
- **Interests**: Journaling, yoga, mindfulness apps, reading about mental health, photography, hiking, self-improvement podcasts
- **Other Important Facts**: Leah has been in therapy for three years, experimenting with techniques like Cognitive Behavioral Therapy (CBT) and mindfulness. She is considering adopting a pet for emotional support.

Detailed Description:

Megan Harper is a 27-year-old marketing coordinator who balances a fast-paced career with a personal journey toward better mental health. Like many young professionals in a demanding industry, Megan frequently experiences anxiety stemming from both work pressures and unresolved family dynamics. She finds herself often overwhelmed by spiraling thoughts that keep her awake at night, leading her to explore various self-help methods. Although she is high-functioning at work, Leah privately struggles with feelings of inadequacy and imposter syndrome, which exacerbate her anxiety.

Megan's personal life is deeply affected by her mental health challenges. After experiencing burnout at her last job, she committed to finding ways to manage her well-being more effectively. She regularly practices yoga and meditation, often using apps like Calm or Headspace to guide her. She has found solace in journaling, particularly when her thoughts feel out of control, and has become a strong advocate for mental health awareness within her friend group. Despite her struggles, Megan is optimistic and driven to improve her quality of life, with aspirations of maintaining a better work-life balance and emotional stability.

Amelie Brooks

Chapter 1: Understanding the Overthinking Phenomenon

Overthinking is a standard part of daily life, often trapping us in endless cycles of thoughts that loop without conclusion. What seems like harmless mental chatter at first can quietly infiltrate our routines and relationships. A seemingly productive examination of details can transform into a burdensome chain, keeping us from decisive actions and peace of mind. For many, this cycle begins with good intentions. A desire to make informed decisions or anticipate future obstacles, but it can quickly become insidious, spreading doubt and anxiety into all areas of life like creeping roots.

The journey into understanding overthinking starts with recognizing how it shows up in everyday situations, often disguised as thorough planning or problem-solving. Yet, such patterns tend to complicate rather than clarify, leading us into traps where the fear of making mistakes thwarts progress. This chapter uncovers the dual nature of these thought processes, their apparent necessity and hidden costs. By highlighting the different types of overthinking, such as worry, self-doubt, and perfectionism, readers gain insight into the varied forms it can take. Armed with this awareness, the chapter invites you to explore ways to discern when thinking shifts from constructive reflection to detrimental rumination, offering perspectives on embracing imperfection and focusing on what truly matters.

How often do you find yourself trapped in overthinking, and what triggers these cycles in your own life?

Definition and Types of Overthinking

When we talk about overthinking, we're diving into a complex web of thoughts that often feels endless and circular. It involves repeatedly pondering choices, events, or possibilities without reaching any resolution. This is commonly referred to as "paralysis by analysis," where the inability to break free from pondering leaves us stuck. Overthinking can be paralyzing because it focuses on what might happen instead of taking action in the present.

Interestingly, overthinking can sometimes manifest in ways that appear productive but are counterproductive. In specific contexts, analyzing every detail might seem like thorough problem-solving, yet it often leads to increased anxiety rather than clarity. For instance, deliberating over every possible outcome of a simple choice, such as what to wear to a social event, becomes an unproductive cycle when it prevents making a decision entirely. It's crucial to recognize that not all detailed thought processes are beneficial, which is critical to understanding the dual nature of overthinking.

There are several forms of overthinking, each with unique traits and effects on our mindset. Worry is a prime example, characterized by persistent concerns about future uncertainties. These can range from small-scale worries, like anticipating a traffic jam, to existential musings, such as fears about long-term happiness or fulfillment. Self-doubt is another form deeply intertwined with one's self-perception, often leading individuals to question their abilities or decisions unnecessarily. Perfectionism is another form where the relentless pursuit of flawlessness hampers progress and fosters indecision.

Cognitive traps play a significant role in perpetuating overthinking. One common trap is catastrophizing, where individuals assume the worst-case scenario will happen. This reality distortion amplifies fears and blinds us to more rational solutions or perspectives. Imagine you're awaiting feedback from a job interview. While it's natural to feel anxious, catastrophizing might lead you to believe you've already failed, triggering feelings of disappointment before receiving any news. Such thinking patterns obscure potential problem-solving avenues, reinforcing negative views and feeding the vicious cycle of overthinking.

Recognizing these forms of overthinking helps us see how they infiltrate daily life. At the same time, some level of reflection is necessary for growth and learning; excessive rumination burdens mental health. Studies suggest that chronic overthinkers may experience heightened stress levels and diminished well-being (Sperber, 2023). It's about more than just overthinking but how those thoughts take control, impacting judgment and emotional stability.

Recognizing when thought processes become cyclical and unproductive is a pivotal guideline for navigating overthinking. Knowing whether the mental effort leads to actionable solutions can help distinguish between constructive reflection and detrimental rumination. If no actionable plan emerges, it may be time to shift focus or employ techniques to break free from these loops and prevent them from masquerading as problem-solving tools.

Another critical approach is understanding the context in which our thoughts operate. Though thoughtful consideration can lead to positive outcomes if applied to areas within our control. Yet, overthinking becomes destructive when focused on variables that are uncertain or beyond immediate influence. By distinguishing between what you can change and cannot, you cultivate a sense of empowerment that fosters healthier mental habits.

Cultivating awareness of these patterns allows individuals to intervene earlier. Recognizing triggers that propel us into overthinking spirals - such as high-pressure situations or personal insecurities - offers an opportunity to apply strategies designed to mitigate their effects. Approaches might include practicing mindfulness, engaging in physical activities, or setting designated times to sort through worries constructively.

While overthinking is interwoven deeply with our cognitive processes, mastering its nuances enables greater control over our thoughts and feelings. This understanding aligns with the journey toward personal growth, where acknowledging and reframing thought patterns contributes significantly to emotional intelligence. By equipping ourselves with overthinking's nature and its various forms, we lay the groundwork for healthier coping strategies and enhanced quality of life.

Reflecting on the definitions and examples, it becomes evident that managing to overthink requires self-awareness and active participation in reshaping our mental landscapes. Essentially, it's not merely about halting the process but transforming how you engage with your thoughts. Recognizing the fine line between analysis and paralysis shifts the narrative, promoting a balanced approach to thinking that supports rather than hinders our pursuit of happiness and peace.

Ultimately, this exploration serves as a reminder that while overthinking may stem from a desire for perfection or certainty, embracing imperfection and uncertainty often leads to more fulfilling outcomes. Understanding and addressing these thought patterns equips individuals with the tools to reduce their grip, paving the way for more mindful and deliberate living.

Can you recognize a recent situation where overthinking prevented you from deciding? How did it affect your outcome?

Symptoms and Signs to Recognize

Recognizing the signs of overthinking in oneself is crucial for fostering early intervention and promoting mental well-being. The psychological symptoms of overthinking often present as racing thoughts, anxiety, and irritability. These symptoms can be relentless, causing a person to feel mentally trapped in an unending cycle of worry and doubt. It's like a song stuck on repeat, creating mental noise that disrupts sleep and strains personal relationships. For example, racing thoughts might keep you at night as you replay conversations or decisions. This emotional turbulence can lead to irritability, affecting interactions with friends and family. When anxious thoughts dominate, individuals may find it challenging to concentrate on tasks, further increasing stress levels.

Overthinking doesn't only affect the mind; its physical manifestations are evidence of the mind-body connection. Stress from constant worrying can lead to tension headaches, where the continuous clenching of muscles around the neck and scalp results in a persistent ache. Fatigue is another common symptom, as the brain's continuous processing leaves the body feeling drained. Imagine waking up just as tired as when you went to bed, your energy sapped by the mental marathon you run daily. These symptoms highlight the profound connection between our psychological and physical states. Stress hormones like cortisol are released in response to perceived threats, whether real or imagined, demonstrating the tangible impact of mental health on our physical condition.

Behavioral changes are another indicator of overthinking. Avoidance and procrastination often emerge as coping mechanisms. Instead of confronting challenges head-on, the overthinker might sidestep them altogether. For instance, someone might delay deciding due to fear of choosing wrong, thus perpetuating a cycle of indecision and worry. Procrastination becomes a temporary escape, providing brief relief from anxiety while ultimately compounding stress when deadlines loom closer without progress. Over time, these behaviors can become ingrained, making it harder to break free from overthinking and take proactive steps.

Social withdrawal is a significant consequence of overthinking that deserves attention. As internal struggles intensify, individuals may pull back from social interactions out of fear of judgment or criticism. They might cancel plans, dodge phone calls, or make excuses to avoid gatherings. This isolation can create a vicious cycle where loneliness amplifies feelings of inadequacy and misunderstanding. Without the support and perspective of others, it's easy to spiral deeper into negative thought patterns. The absence of social engagement deprives individuals of necessary emotional validation and connection, highlighting the importance of maintaining interpersonal awareness. Engaging in open conversations and reaching out to trusted friends or family can help bridge the gap between internal turmoil and external reality, offering a lifeline to those engulfed in their thoughts.

Recognizing these signs - psychological symptoms, physical manifestations, behavioral changes, and social withdrawal - makes it evident how pervasive the impact of overthinking can be. Each aspect informs the other, creating a comprehensive picture of how destructive unchecked thoughts can become. However, identifying these signs paves the way for intervention. By acknowledging that overthinking affects various aspects of life, individuals can begin to adopt strategies to manage their mental health effectively.

Mindfulness practices, such as meditation and deep breathing exercises, can be valuable tools in combating overthinking. These techniques encourage individuals to remain present, breaking free from the habitual clutches of past regrets and future anxieties. For instance, dedicating a few minutes daily to focus on one's breath can provide a profound sense of calm and clarity. Grounding exercises help minimize the grip of overwhelming thoughts, granting individuals respite and renewed perspective.

Sometimes, setting aside specific times to reflect on worries can prevent them from spilling over into every moment. Scheduling this "worry time" might seem counterintuitive, but it allows one to acknowledge concerns within a structured framework, reducing their power throughout the day. Journaling is another effective method. Writing down thoughts and feelings helps externalize internal chaos, making it easier to process emotions objectively. Putting pen to paper also serves as a release, a cathartic experience that offers insight into recurring thought patterns.

Additionally, seeking professional guidance through therapy or counseling can provide tailored support and coping mechanisms suited to individual needs. Cognitive-behavioral therapy (CBT), a form of talk therapy that focuses on modifying negative thought patterns, is particularly beneficial for overthinkers. It alters negative thought patterns and develops healthier responses to stress. Therapists can guide individuals in identifying cognitive distortions, challenging irrational beliefs, and fostering resilience against overthinking triggers.

Lastly, maintaining strong social connections is vital in curbing the effects of overthinking. Friends and family can offer reassurance and alternative perspectives and remind individuals of their strengths. Encouraging open dialogue about mental health normalizes these discussions, creating safe spaces for vulnerability and growth. By fostering supportive networks, individuals gain allies in their journey toward mental well-being.

Have you noticed any of these symptoms in your own life? What steps can you take to break free from the cycle of overthinking?

Impact on Mental Well-Being

Overthinking is an all-too-familiar companion for many, weaving itself into the fabric of daily life and significantly impacting emotional health. One of the most pronounced consequences of overthinking is its link to increased anxiety and depression. The constant cycle of worry consumes the mind, creating a breeding ground for feelings of hopelessness. Such feelings are not merely fleeting; they can become entrenched in one's psyche, leading to a state of chronic anxiety or even depression. Over time, these negative emotions can chip away at an individual's well-being, robbing them of joy and fulfillment.

The relentless nature of overthinking often clouds cognitive clarity. Imagine navigating through dense fog—every step is uncertain, every decision fraught with hesitation. This mental fog can overload the brain, hindering the ability to process information effectively. As clarity diminishes, decision-making becomes increasingly complex, making individuals indecisive and second-guessing. Whether trivial or significant, choices become burdensome tasks that exacerbate stress levels. The mind becomes a tangled web of thoughts, each thread pulling us further from resolution.

Personal relationships, too, suffer under the weight of overthinking. Miscommunication and assumptions become frequent visitors in conversations. When our minds are preoccupied with endless scenarios and potential outcomes, it's challenging to communicate clearly and listen actively. Assumptions about others' intentions or feelings can quickly arise from this muddled thinking, leading to misunderstandings.

These missteps can strain relationships, creating distance and tension where connection and understanding should exist. This highlights the need for clearer thinking and open communication to foster healthy relationships.

To mitigate the detrimental effects of overthinking, reframing thought patterns is crucial. Cognitive traps loom large for those who overthink, drawing individuals into distorted realities. Awareness of these traps is critical to disrupting ingrained patterns of thought. Individuals can distance themselves from their harmful impact by naming these distortions and recognizing when they occur. This practice empowers individuals to take control of their thoughts and steer them towards healthier avenues.

Reframing often involves actively challenging negative thoughts and replacing them with balanced, realistic perspectives. It requires conscious effort and patience, but the rewards are immense. A clearer mind and a healthier emotional state. For example, focusing on potential solutions and positive outcomes can provide much-needed relief and comfort instead of dwelling on worst-case scenarios. This shift in perspective not only alleviates stress but also encourages proactive problem-solving, turning what was once a source of anxiety into an opportunity for growth.

Another effective strategy is seeking support from friends, family, or professionals. Sharing worries and perspectives with others can offer valuable insights and alleviate the burden of carrying everything alone. It provides a different lens through which to view situations, helping to break the cycle of overthinking. Meditation or journaling can be powerful tools to calm the mind and organize scattered thoughts, fostering a sense of peace and control.

It's essential to create an environment conducive to mental clarity. This might involve setting boundaries around social media consumption, ensuring adequate rest, and maintaining a balanced lifestyle. Physical well-being is crucial in supporting mental health, so regular exercise, a nutritious diet, and sufficient sleep should not be overlooked. These habits nourish both body and mind, providing a solid foundation for emotional resilience.

Remember, while overthinking presents challenges, overcoming them is entirely within your reach with dedication and the right strategies. You can reclaim your emotional health by recognizing the traps of overthinking and actively reframing thoughts. Doing so improves decision-making capabilities and enhances relationships, enabling individuals to lead fuller, more engaged lives.

How has overthinking impacted your emotional well-being or relationships, and what can you do to reframe your thought patterns?

Consequences on Physical Health

Overthinking is more than a mental struggle; it profoundly impacts physical health, linking our minds and bodies in ways you might not always perceive. At its core, chronic overthinking activates the body's stress response system - the fight-or-flight mechanism - designed to protect us from immediate danger.

However, this system can harm rather than heal when constantly engaged through persistent worrying and rumination.

Its sustained stress response due to overthinking often results in fatigue. The body remains in a heightened state of alertness, using significant energy reserves without allowing for recovery. This constant pressure depletes energy levels, leading to exhaustion and burnout. Imagine running a marathon without ever stopping. That's essentially what the body endures during prolonged overthinking episodes.

Insomnia is another common issue associated with overthinking. Sleep becomes elusive as the mind races with thoughts late into the night. This lack of rest further compounds stress, creating a vicious cycle that undermines physical wellness. The sleepless nights eventually take their toll, disrupting the natural circadian rhythm and affecting mood, concentration, and overall functioning during the day.

Moreover, the link between overthinking and cardiovascular problems is gaining attention. Research indicates that persistent anxiety and worry increase the risk of heart-related issues. Stress hormones like cortisol elevate blood pressure and heart rate, increasing the risk of heart-related problems (Renoir et al., 2013). The connection isn't merely coincidental; it demonstrates how mental processes influence bodily health.

Neglecting self-care is another critical aspect influenced by overthinking. When consumed by incessant thoughts, individuals often forgo basic self-care routines. Eating habits may suffer through overeating unhealthy foods as comfort or forgetting meals entirely. Similarly, social habits also change; the mind preoccupied with worries finds little room for social interactions, which are essential for emotional well-being. This lack of balance in diet and social activities contributes significantly to declining physical health.

Maintaining mindfulness practices holds promise as a powerful counterbalance to these adverse effects. Mindfulness encourages living in the present moment, breaking the chains of relentless overthinking. Individuals can reduce the automatic stress reactions tied to their worries by focusing on the here and now. Techniques such as meditation, deep breathing, and mindful movement help recalibrate the nervous system away from stress-induced patterns.

Furthermore, recognizing triggers of overthinking allows for proactive management. Understanding the situations or thoughts that incite excessive rumination enables individuals to address them before they spiral out of control. Cognitive-behavioral strategies can be helpful here, as they provide tools to reframe negative thought patterns and encourage healthier, more realistic perspectives.

Adopting a holistic approach to managing mind and body health is crucial in mitigating the physical consequences of overthinking. It involves integrating regular physical activity, balanced nutrition, adequate sleep, and mindfulness practices into everyday life. Physical exercise, in particular, is a great stress reliever, releasing endorphins that naturally improve mood and decrease stress perception.

Developing a routine that prioritizes self-care fosters resilience against the pressures of overthinking. Simple actions like taking short breaks during work, setting aside time for hobbies, and engaging in social activities can significantly alter how stress is managed daily. These activities offer outlets for relieving mental strain, allowing for moments of joy and relaxation.

Creating awareness about the intricate connections between our thoughts and physical states empowers individuals to take charge of their health more comprehensively. Understanding that the mind doesn't operate in isolation but interacts dynamically with every part of us drives home the importance of caring for both aspects equally.

How has overthinking affected your physical health, and what changes can you make to balance your mind and body?

Insights and Implications

In navigating the complexities of overthinking, this chapter unveils how it entwines our everyday lives, often overshadowing mental clarity and emotional well-being. Through exploration of its different forms - from worries about daily uncertainties to self-doubt and perfectionism - you see how these thoughts cycle in our minds, sometimes blurring into anxiety and fear instead of offering resolution. Recognizing these patterns is essential, as it allows us to intervene, preventing our minds from falling into relentless loops that only heighten stress. It's like learning to identify a storm brewing at sea so you can find shelter before it hits.

As you reflect on these insights, the journey encourages you to reclaim that balance by understanding what you can control and letting go of what remains uncertain. This newfound awareness empowers us to transform our cognitive landscapes, promoting healthier coping strategies and enriching our quality of life.

Whether practicing mindfulness or seeking external support, taking proactive steps allows us to step back and view our thoughts with clarity, fostering emotional intelligence. By embracing imperfection and cherishing moments of stillness, you learn to navigate life's challenges more mindfully, paving the way toward lasting peace and joy.

What small steps can you take today to regain control over your thoughts and foster a more mindful approach to life's challenges?

Here is what Megan learned from reading the chapter:

Megan realized just how much overthinking has been impacting her day-to-day life. The constant mental loops, particularly her self-doubt and perfectionism, often leave her feeling drained and stuck. She was surprised by how easily overthinking disguises itself as productive planning, like when she replays work conversations repeatedly in her head or worries endlessly about small details in her personal life.

What hit home for Megan was the concept of "paralysis by analysis." She often finds herself caught between wanting to make the right decision and being afraid to make any decision, ultimately leading to inaction. She could relate to catastrophizing, especially when waiting for feedback on work projects or social interactions. Recognizing these patterns in herself helped her feel a sense of relief, knowing she's not alone and that overthinking can take many forms.

One of Megan's biggest takeaways was the need to distinguish between constructive reflection and detrimental rumination.

The idea of setting "worry time" resonated with her, as she's often overwhelmed by her thoughts throughout the day, making it hard to concentrate. By permitting herself to address her worries in a structured way, she could see how this might free up mental space and allow her to focus better during work.

In terms of action steps, Megan plans to start small. She'll practice identifying when her thoughts shift from problem-solving to unproductive worry. She'll also begin incorporating more mindfulness techniques, like setting aside five minutes for deep breathing when she feels the onset of anxious thoughts. She's also thinking about revisiting her journaling habit to capture and release those racing thoughts, helping her break the overthinking cycle.

This chapter reminded Megan that managing to overthink isn't about shutting down her thoughts but transforming how she engages with them. She feels encouraged to approach her mental health journey with more compassion and to embrace the imperfection and uncertainty that life inevitably brings.

Chapter 2: Discovering Mindfulness: From Ancient Wisdom to Modern Practice

Discovering mindfulness is like embarking on a journey to understand our minds. It combines ancient wisdom with modern insights, offering a serene alternative to the chaos in our thoughts. For centuries, mindfulness has invited us to observe life as it unfolds, moment by moment. Today, this practice is experiencing a renaissance, finding its place in contemporary psychology as both an antidote to overthinking and a means to enhance our overall quality of life. In a world where our thoughts often run rampant, grasping the essence of mindfulness provides a reprieve. A way to reclaim peace amid the turmoil.

Within this chapter, you venture into the heart of mindfulness, exploring its role as a formidable tool against the mind's constant chatter. You trace its journey from ancient philosophies to its pivotal integration into modern therapeutic practices, examining how it has transformed into a widely acclaimed method for improving mental health. Readers will delve into the techniques that anchor mindfulness in everyday life, learning how these practices can counteract anxiety and stress. This chapter promises to illuminate how mindfulness can be seamlessly woven into our daily routines, offering practical solutions for personal growth and emotional resilience by unpacking the core principles and dispelling common misconceptions.

How could incorporating mindfulness into your daily life help you navigate the mental chaos you experience?

Historical Origins of Mindfulness

Mindfulness, a concept rooted in ancient Buddhist traditions, serves as a spiritual and practical tool for enlightenment by cultivating awareness and presence. Originally, mindfulness was part of a broader Buddhist system aimed at liberation from suffering (Keng et al., 2011). This traditional perspective views mindfulness as interconnected with other practices, such as ethics and meditation, necessary for achieving deep spiritual insights and liberation. Practitioners were encouraged to be mindful of their bodies, feelings, and thoughts, reflecting on teachings like impermanence and non-self (Keng et al., 2011).

As mindfulness practices evolved over centuries, they began to transcend cultural boundaries, entering Western societies during the 20th century. Jon Kabat-Zinn was pivotal in this transition; they integrated Eastern mindfulness concepts into Western psychology. Mindfulness-Based Stress Reduction (MBSR), an eight-week program developed by Jon Kabat-Zinn, teaches mindfulness meditation to help manage stress. The MBSR program, developed at the University of Massachusetts Medical School, offered an eight-week regimen to help individuals manage stress more effectively. Integrating Eastern wisdom with scientific frameworks played a crucial role in popularizing mindfulness in the West, particularly among those more accustomed to scientific methodologies than religious philosophies (Selva, 2017).

Adopting mindfulness within Western contexts wasn't merely replicating Eastern traditions; it necessitated adaptations to suit modern lifestyles. Traditional methods were simplified to align with everyday life, making mindfulness more accessible to a broader audience. Research has substantiated the cognitive benefits of these practices, highlighting their efficacy in enhancing emotional regulation and promoting psychological well-being. Studies within clinical psychology underscore two main components of mindfulness: the self-regulation of attention and a specific attitude toward experiences characterized by curiosity and acceptance (Keng et al., 2011).

In contemporary practice, mindfulness has become a global movement, garnering significant attention from health professionals worldwide. Its prevalence in therapeutic settings is notable, with many professionals utilizing mindfulness techniques to address various mental health challenges, including anxiety and depression. This widespread interest is underscored by research linking consistent mindfulness practice to changes in brain structure and function, particularly areas involved in emotional regulation and resilience.

Mindfulness's global recognition is not limited to therapeutic environments but extends into various aspects of daily life, appealing to a diverse range of individuals seeking personal development. Its versatility allows it to be adapted across different cultures and lifestyles, demonstrating its universal applicability. Whether practiced as part of formal meditation sessions, integrated into daily activities, or employed as a strategy for coping with life's stressors, mindfulness offers practical tools for enhancing one's quality of life.

What aspects of mindfulness's journey from ancient traditions to modern practices resonate most with your current mental health challenges?

Mindfulness in Modern Psychology

Mindfulness is a powerful tool to manage overthinking, anxiety, and depression. In recent years, an extensive body of research has brought mindfulness into the domain of psychological frameworks, illustrating its role in fostering emotional resilience and reducing mental distress.

Numerous studies highlight how mindfulness practice leads to significant reductions in anxiety and depression, often by facilitating changes in brain structures associated with emotional regulation. Regular mindfulness meditation can strengthen brain areas involved in attention and self-regulation. This structural enhancement supports improved emotional control, helping individuals navigate their thoughts and emotions without becoming overwhelmed. By changing how you process emotions, mindfulness cultivates mental calmness, helping us face life's challenges more effectively.

Beyond its standalone benefits, mindfulness is a valuable complement to cognitive-behavioral therapy (CBT), particularly in managing cycles of negative thinking. CBT aims to change maladaptive thought patterns, and mindfulness aids this process by promoting awareness and acceptance of one's immediate experience. By observing thoughts non-judgmentally, individuals can disrupt automatic adverse reactions, allowing them to respond to situations with greater clarity and composure. The synergy between mindfulness and CBT enhances therapeutic outcomes, offering a robust framework for tackling the root causes of overthinking.

Mindfulness also proves instrumental as a preventive measure against stress and anxiety across various populations.

Consistent practice fosters resilience, equipping individuals to handle life's pressures more easily. By training the mind to focus on present-moment experiences rather than ruminating over past or future worries, mindfulness helps reduce stress levels. This shift in focus not only alleviates current anxiety but also builds a more resilient mental state that can withstand future stressors. In educational settings, for example, mindfulness programs have shown promise in helping students cope with academic pressures, leading to enhanced performance and well-being.

Real-world applications further attest to mindfulness's effectiveness, demonstrated through therapeutic settings and personal testimonials. Many therapists integrate mindfulness into their practices, observing firsthand how it aids clients in achieving better mental health. Evidence from controlled trials corroborates these observations, indicating that mindfulness-based interventions like Mindfulness-Based Stress Reduction (MBSR) and Mindfulness-Based Cognitive Therapy (MBCT) effectively decrease symptoms of anxiety and depression.

Individual stories also illuminate the transformative impact of mindfulness. People who incorporate mindful practices into their daily lives often report a newfound ability to manage overwhelming thoughts, improving overall quality of life. These personal narratives underscore the accessibility and universality of mindfulness; they offer tools not just for those facing psychological challenges but also for anyone seeking to enhance their emotional intelligence and coping mechanisms.

How might practicing mindfulness help you manage your own overthinking or emotional stress?

Core Principles and Practices of Mindfulness

Our minds often dwell on the past or worry about the future in our fast-paced world. This cycle can lead to anxiety, diminishing our quality of life. Mindfulness is a powerful tool to manage these intrusive thoughts by emphasizing the art of living in the present moment. By anchoring ourselves in the present, we reduce rumination and fully appreciate daily experiences.

Mindfulness is not just about being present; it also involves observing oneself without judgment. This non-judgmental observation helps foster a compassionate relationship with oneself, where thoughts are viewed as passing phenomena rather than permanent fixtures. By viewing thoughts as temporary, you cultivate mental clarity and inner peace. This approach encourages acceptance, recognizing our thoughts and emotions without labeling them as good or bad, offering a gentle reminder that self-compassion aids emotional resilience.

Techniques like mindful breathing and body scanning are fundamental to mindfulness practice, both of which serve as anchors for our attention. Mindful breathing involves focusing on the breath and noticing its rhythmic ebb and flow. At the same time, body scanning entails a mental journey through the body, tuning into physical sensations without attempting to alter them. These practices help bring our attention back to the present whenever the mind wanders, supporting psychological well-being. Over time, they help form neural pathways that enhance self-regulation and reduce impulsivity.

Integrating mindfulness into our daily activities transforms routine tasks into moments of awareness and contemplation.

Activities such as washing dishes, walking, or eating can become mindful exercises, inviting complete immersion and focus. Consider eating mindfully, where you savor each bite, appreciating flavors and textures with intention. This integration deepens our appreciation for simple tasks and bolsters our ability to remain present amidst the busyness of life. Therefore, even mundane chores provide opportunities for practicing mindfulness, infusing them with purpose and presence.

Present-moment awareness is crucial in combating overthinking. It encourages us to shift our focus from what was or what might be, directing it instead toward what is happening right now. For instance, when sipping a warm cup of tea, notice the color, aroma, and warmth. By doing so, you build a habit of engaging fully with your current experience, which can markedly reduce anxiety levels fueled by hypothetical scenarios. Such practice helps break the habit of mindlessly drifting away from the present, grounding us in reality with a clearer perspective.

Non-judgmental observation extends beyond mere awareness; it embraces a mindset that is open and accepting of all experiences. Imagine watching clouds float across the sky, some thick and dark, others light and fluffy. Similarly, thoughts drift through the mind, and with non-judgmental observation, you learn to watch them come and go without attachment or aversion. This exercise heightens self-awareness and nurtures a balanced outlook, helping dissolve fear or bias associated with specific thoughts.

Techniques like mindful breathing and body scanning play a vital role in establishing a mindfulness practice. They are simple yet profoundly effective methods for redirecting our focus from stressors to a state of calm. In mindful breathing, focus on each inhale and exhale, noting how the chest rises and falls. In body scanning, systematically attend to parts of the body, acknowledging tension or relaxation without judgment. These practices anchor us, offering solace during overwhelming times and teaching us the skill of conscious redirection from stress to serenity.

The seamless integration of mindfulness into everyday life is transformative, converting ordinary tasks into avenues of self-reflection and heightened awareness. Once a mechanical function, walking becomes a deliberate exercise in feeling each step, the earth beneath your feet, and the rhythm of movement. Similarly, cleaning transforms into a ritual of purifying both space and mind. By weaving mindfulness into daily routines, you enrich our lives with a tapestry of intentionality and awareness, promoting sustained mental and emotional health.

In what areas of your daily routine could you begin to apply mindfulness techniques to improve your emotional well-being?

Common Misconceptions Clarified

The exploration of mindfulness often stirs a variety of misconceptions that can deter individuals from embracing its full potential. One common myth is the confusion between mindfulness and formal meditation, leading to the belief that only structured sessions qualify as mindful practice. While traditional meditation involves specific routines and settings, mindfulness extends beyond these boundaries and is accessible anytime. For instance, one can cultivate mindfulness while performing simple tasks like eating or walking by focusing on the immediate sensory experiences. This broader accessibility allows mindfulness to seamlessly fit into diverse lifestyles without needing designated meditation time, making it a versatile tool for managing to overthink.

Another common misconception is that mindfulness is an escape from reality when it encourages us to face challenges with clarity. In contrast, true mindfulness encourages individuals to face their challenges head-on with clarity and presence. People can develop greater resilience and emotional intelligence by acknowledging thoughts and emotions without judgment. This process of confronting rather than avoiding discomfort helps individuals understand their reactions and triggers, enabling them to respond thoughtfully to life's challenges. Over time, this practice builds a sturdy foundation for personal growth, allowing individuals to navigate the complexities of their emotions with ease and composure.

Additionally, thinking that mindfulness is a quick fix is misleading. Like any skill, mastering mindfulness requires consistent and patient practice. The positive outcomes associated with mindfulness, such as reduced anxiety and improved well-being, are not instantaneous but emerge through gradual development over time. Consistent dedication to mindfulness fosters deeper self-awareness and enhances one's ability to remain present under stress. As individuals consistently engage in mindfulness, they notice subtle shifts in their thought patterns and emotional responses, contributing to long-term psychological benefits.

Mindfulness is also mistakenly seen as exclusive to spiritual people but accessible to everyone. Contrary to this belief, mindfulness is universally applicable and inclusive, available to anyone regardless of spiritual beliefs or background. It is not a religious practice but a secular approach to cultivating awareness and attention in everyday life. Mindfulness transcends cultural and religious boundaries, welcoming individuals from all walks of life to explore its benefits. This inclusivity makes mindfulness a valuable resource in various contexts, including workplaces, educational institutions, and therapeutic settings, where people seek effective strategies to cope with stress and enhance well-being.

In addressing these myths, it becomes evident that mindfulness can be integrated into daily routines without requiring drastic lifestyle changes. Its adaptability ensures that individuals can engage with mindfulness practices at their own pace, gradually incorporating them into their lives. By debunking these misconceptions, you open the door for more people to explore the benefits of mindfulness, enabling them to harness its power for personal transformation and mental clarity.

Through understanding and dismantling these myths, mindfulness emerges as an empowering practice that supports mental health and emotional well-being. It encourages individuals to live with greater intention and presence, nurturing a sense of calm amid the chaos of modern life. As more people embrace mindfulness with openness and dedication, its potential to transform individual lives and communities becomes increasingly apparent.

Which misconceptions about mindfulness have held you back from fully embracing its potential, and how can you now approach it with an open mind?

Concluding Thoughts

Our exploration reveals that mindfulness offers more than a temporary escape from overthinking, it provides lasting tools for peace and clarity. Mindfulness invites us to anchor ourselves in the present, countering the relentless cycle of worry and rumination that often accompanies modern life. You learn to view your thoughts as fleeting clouds rather than immovable storms through simple yet profound techniques like mindful breathing and non-judgmental observation. This perspective nurtures a compassionate relationship with ourselves, fostering emotional resilience and clarity. As mindfulness seamlessly weaves itself into daily routines, even mundane tasks hold the potential for reflection and self-discovery.

Embracing mindfulness is not about escaping reality but facing life's challenges with intention and peace. The research underscores its transformative impact on mental health, demonstrating how consistent practice can enhance emotional regulation and reduce anxiety. Unlike misconceptions suggest, mindfulness is accessible to everyone, regardless of spiritual inclination or lifestyle. It provides a versatile framework that adapts to diverse needs in therapeutic settings or everyday life. By integrating mindfulness into our lives, you cultivate inner calm, empowering us to navigate our emotions and experiences more efficiently.

What steps can you take today to integrate mindfulness into your life and foster a greater sense of calm and emotional resilience?

Here is what Megan learned from reading the chapter:

Megan found that this chapter on mindfulness deeply resonated with her ongoing struggles with overthinking. The concept of being present at the moment was particularly eye-opening, as she often finds herself caught between worrying about the future and replaying past events. This constant mental chatter is something she's been working to manage, and learning that mindfulness has been used for centuries and is now integrated into modern psychology helped her see the practice in a new light. It reassured her that there is both wisdom and evidence behind mindfulness as a tool for improving mental well-being.

One of the most significant takeaways for Megan was the realization that mindfulness doesn't have to be formal meditation. She had previously believed it required long, structured sessions, but this chapter showed her how mindfulness can be woven into everyday activities. Simple tasks like focusing on her breath, paying attention while drinking tea, or walking became opportunities to practice mindfulness. This approach felt more achievable for Megan, who sometimes feels intimidated by formal meditation.

Megan also connected with using mindfulness to shift her focus away from overthinking and toward the present moment. After reading about mindful breathing, she tried it and noticed how calming it was, even after just a few minutes. This experience showed her that with practice, mindfulness could help her handle stress and anxiety more effectively—especially when she tends to spiral into perfectionism or catastrophizing. She reflected on how this mindfulness practice tied into what she learned in the previous chapter about overthinking cycles, seeing mindfulness as a practical way to interrupt those patterns.

Another aspect that struck Megan was the emphasis on non-judgmental observation of thoughts. Often, she is critical of herself when she gets overwhelmed, and this chapter helped her understand the importance of observing her thoughts without the need to fix them immediately. This non-judgmental approach is something Megan wants to apply more in her life, as it could help her develop a more compassionate relationship with herself during stressful times.

Incorporating mindfulness into her daily life now feels like a tangible goal for Megan. She plans to continue using mindful breathing and other techniques to help ground herself during moments of stress. Whether she's walking, working, or simply enjoying a cup of tea, Megan sees mindfulness as a tool to manage her overthinking and foster a sense of peace and clarity in her everyday life.

Chapter 3: Mindful Breathing Techniques

Mindful breathing offers a path to calm and balance in our fast-paced world. It invites us to focus on the rhythm of our breath, providing a retreat from the demands of modern life. This chapter introduces mindful breathing as a valuable ally. A readily available tool to center our thoughts and emotions amid daily stressors. It's not just about taking a deep breath; it's about finding tranquility amidst the chaos that often surrounds us. This introduction aims to spark curiosity about how such a simple act can lead to profound inner peace.

This chapter dives into various techniques of mindful breathing that can be easily incorporated into your routine. You'll learn about breathing exercises designed to anchor you in the present moment and reduce anxiety. From focusing on each inhale and exhale to more structured methods like diaphragmatic breathing or the 4-7-8 technique, these tools are presented with empathy to guide you toward mindfulness gently. The chapter promises practical insights and step-by-step approaches, encouraging personal exploration for those seeking growth and emotional resilience. Whether at the start of your mindfulness journey or looking to deepen your practice, this chapter provides actionable strategies to enrich your mental well-being.

How might incorporating mindful breathing into your daily routine help you find calm amid the stressors of your life?

Amelie Brooks

Basics of Mindful Breathing

Mindful breathing is a transformative practice that significantly impacts our mental well-being. At its core, it involves focusing on the breath with purposeful attention and awareness. This seemingly basic act serves as a grounding technique that helps interrupt cycles of overthinking, which can often lead to anxiety and stress.

Awareness of our breath is an anchor amid our thoughts' stormy seas. When our minds become overwhelmed with racing thoughts, returning focus to the natural rhythm of inhalation and exhalation can provide stability. Being mindful of each breath encourages us to live in the present moment, detaching from the clutter of past regrets or future anxieties. For example, envision yourself sitting quietly, eyes gently closed, noticing the air entering and leaving your body. Each inhale brings in calmness, and each exhale releases tension.

Please take a look at how your breathing changes with your emotional states. Recognizing these patterns can offer valuable insights into what might be triggering stress or anxiety. Typically, when a person is tense or anxious, their breaths become shallow and rapid, often using the upper chest rather than the diaphragm. Conversely, slow, deep breaths signal relaxation and peace. By consciously observing how you breathe in different situations, you can gain awareness of what causes distress, enabling you to manage your reactions more effectively. Imagine a time when you felt incredibly stressed. Try recalling how your breath thought then; was it constricted and hurried?

Moreover, understanding these patterns provides an opportunity to make deliberate changes. A study (Department of Health & Human Services, 2015) has shown that shifting from shallow to more profound abdominal breaths can ease muscular tension and promote overall relaxation. If you've ever practiced yoga or meditation, you've likely experienced this powerful connection between breath control and emotional balance.

The beauty of mindful breathing lies in its simplicity; it doesn't require special techniques or extensive training. You don't have to sit cross-legged on a cushion for hours or adhere to strict protocols. Instead, you can bring attention to your breath wherever you are. Whether seated at your desk, standing in line, or lying in bed, conscious breathing is always accessible. This exercise's simplicity makes it appealing and adaptable, fitting seamlessly into any lifestyle.

Consider starting with just five minutes a day. Find a quiet space, and sit comfortably. Please close your eyes and note how the air feels as it enters your nose, fills your lungs, and exits through your mouth. Focus solely on this sensation. If your mind wanders - a perfectly regular occurrence - gently redirect your attention back to your breath without judgment. This repeated redirection enhances mindfulness by cultivating concentration and presence.

Beyond individual practice, mindful breathing can complement other therapeutic approaches. It's a staple component in both cognitive behavioral therapy (CBT) and dialectical behavior therapy (DBT), known to improve outcomes for those struggling with anxiety and depression (Telloian, 2021). Research highlights how combining these therapies with mindful breathing techniques can empower individuals to navigate emotional challenges more effectively. For instance, one study demonstrated that veterans practicing mindfulness-based stress reduction, including breathing exercises, reported lowered depression levels and improved coping mechanisms.

Mindful breathing isn't just about reducing stress; it also fosters emotional intelligence. Fostering self-awareness allows you to understand better and manage your emotions. Enhanced emotional regulation is critical to personal growth, helping you respond to life's stressors more resiliently.

Can you recall when focusing on your breath helped you regain control of your emotions? How could this practice support you in future stressful situations?

Deep-Breathing Techniques

Many people feel overwhelmed by stress and anxiety in modern life. Deep breathing techniques offer a sanctuary of calm to navigate these turbulent emotions. Practicing diaphragmatic breathing, box breathing, and the 4-7-8 method can transform your mental state, bringing tranquility and focus.

Diaphragmatic breathing, often called belly breathing, is a fundamental exercise that increases breath efficiency by engaging the diaphragm. This technique not only enhances oxygen flow but also encourages relaxation and clarity. With diaphragmatic breathing, focus on your abdomen's movement instead of your chest's. Begin by finding a comfortable seated or lying position. Place one hand on your chest and the other on your abdomen. Inhale deeply through your nose, allowing your diaphragm to expand fully and push your hand outward while keeping your chest still. As you exhale slowly through pursed lips, feel your abdomen contract. Initially, this might take some practice, but it becomes second nature over time. This type of breathing encourages better oxygen exchange, which can help reduce tension and elevate mental clarity. Studies show that diaphragmatic breathing can decrease stress by lowering cortisol levels, fostering a sense of well-being.

Box breathing, another effective technique, centers on creating a rhythmic pattern with each breath. It can serve as an anchor for the mind, helping to quiet racing thoughts and induce a state of focus. Box breathing consists of four equal parts: inhaling, holding, exhaling, and pausing again for the same length. Typically, one might start with a count of four seconds for each part. Begin by sitting comfortably with your back straight. Inhale through your nose for a count of four, feeling the air fill your lungs. Hold your breath for a count of four, then exhale gently through your mouth over four counts. Finally, pause and hold your breath out for a count of four before beginning the cycle anew. You may adjust the count based on your comfort level, but maintaining equal measures is crucial. This method not only helps slow down the breath but also brings a heightened awareness of the present moment, which can dramatically reduce anxiety. Box breathing is used by professionals like Navy SEALs, demonstrating its effectiveness in inducing calm under pressure.

The 4-7-8 breathing technique, developed by Dr. Andrew Weil, is particularly effective for calming the nervous system and preparing the body for rest. This technique involves a distinct pattern that elongates the breath, maximizing the body's relaxation response. To practice 4-7-8 breathing, sit with a straight back or lie down. Place the tip of your tongue against the ridge of tissue behind your upper front teeth. With your mouth closed, inhale quietly through your nose to a mental count of four. Hold your breath for a count of seven. Exhale completely through your mouth, making a whoosh sound for eight counts. This constitutes one cycle, with four recommended cycles, especially in the beginning stages. The structured pattern prompts the autonomic nervous system to shift from sympathetic (fight-or-flight) activation to parasympathetic (rest-and-digest) mode, promoting a profound calm state. Regular practice of 4-7-8 breathing can improve sleep quality, decrease anxiety, and manage stress more effectively (Brennan, 2021).

When practiced consistently, each of these breathing exercises offers unique benefits that contribute to a quieter mind and a more relaxed body. They act as empowerment tools, granting individuals control over their emotional states regardless of external circumstances. Integrating these techniques into daily routines can lead to lasting improvements in mental health, providing a reliable refuge amidst life's demands.

It's essential to approach these practices with patience and openness. Deep-breathing exercises require persistence, but the rewards are well worth the effort. Over time, as you become more familiar with the rhythms of your breath, you will notice a shift in how you respond to stress and anxiety. Simple adjustments, like incorporating deep-breathing sessions into morning rituals or using them during breaks at work, can make a significant difference. For individuals drawn to personal growth and self-development, these practices enhance emotional intelligence by fostering greater self-awareness and resilience.

Numerous apps and resources are available for those just starting or seeking guidance to facilitate practice and maintain consistency. Applications designed for mindfulness and meditation can provide reminders and instructions to ensure you use these techniques regularly and correctly. In our fast-paced world, where stressors are constant and pervasive, the simplicity and accessibility of deep breathing exercises offer hope and healing.

Which deep-breathing technique resonates with you the most, and how can you start integrating it into your routine to manage stress more effectively?

Using Breaths to Reduce Stress

Recognizing the connection between our physical responses and emotions is critical to understanding how intentional breathing alleviates stress. When faced with stressful situations, our bodies often switch into a 'fight or flight' mode, a response characterized by shallow and rapid breathing. This reaction, while instinctual, can exacerbate feelings of anxiety and stress if not curbed. Understanding this lets you appreciate how changing your breathing directly impacts your emotional well-being.

Mindful breathing is an anchor, grounding us in the present moment and increasing resilience to stress. This meditative practice encourages the individual to focus solely on their breath, serving as a tool to interrupt the relentless cycle of stress-inducing thoughts. In moments where anxiety threatens to disrupt mental clarity, a few minutes of mindful breathing can act as a sanctuary, providing calmness amidst chaos. Integrating such practice into daily routines ensures one is better equipped to handle stress, effectively reducing its grip over time.

Practicing breath control empowers you during life's challenging moments. Those who consistently use regulated breathing techniques report a greater sense of calm and control when confronted with stressful scenarios. Through regular practice, the body becomes accustomed to switching from a state of stress to one of relaxation more swiftly. For example, when dealing with high-pressure projects at work, taking a few moments to engage in deep, controlled breathing can reset one's perspective, allowing for clearer thinking and decision-making.

Controlled breathing stems from the idea that you can intentionally modulate your physical responses. You can lower heart rates and reduce stress hormones like cortisol by consciously slowing down your breathing. Studies have shown that consistent practice of slow and deep breaths fosters emotional stability and offers numerous health benefits like improved immune function and reduced blood pressure.

Incorporating mindful breathing into everyday life does not demand significant effort; instead, it requires a commitment to practice. Simple exercises like the 4-7-8 technique can be seamlessly integrated into daily routines. This method involves inhaling through the nose for four counts, holding the breath for seven, and exhaling through the mouth for eight counts. Such a structured approach gives individuals a tangible way to cope with stress, providing immediate relief and long-term emotional balance.

Moreover, the Box Breathing technique can be an excellent guideline for those seeking a straightforward approach. It encompasses inhaling slowly for four seconds, holding the breath for another four, exhaling steadily for four, and pausing before the next inhale. This cyclical pattern soothes the nervous system and promotes enhanced concentration and mental clarity.

As people become more proficient in mindful breathing practices, they cultivate a more substantial capacity to remain centered amid adversity. Regular breathing exercises reduce stress and promote personal growth, helping you navigate life's challenges more effectively. When practiced regularly, mindfulness transforms how individuals perceive stress, turning it from an overwhelming force into a manageable component of life.

Intentional breathing works like a lens, reshaping perspectives and making the intangible nature of stress more approachable. Each deliberate breath serves as a metaphorical and literal break from tension, illustrating the power one holds in regulating one's physiological and emotional responses. By mastering these techniques, individuals equip themselves with a valuable toolset that strengthens their overall well-being, enabling them to lead more balanced and fulfilling lives.

Guidelines are particularly beneficial for beginners. Establishing a routine practice time, associating breathwork with particular activities, or using reminders such as smartphone apps can facilitate habit formation. While developing a sustained practice may take time, the transformative effects on stress management and emotional intelligence are worth the effort.

How could learning to control your breath during moments of stress change how you handle challenges in your personal or professional life?

Integrating Breathing into Daily Routine

Integrating mindful breathing into daily life enhances mental well-being and reduces stress. It's essential to establish a consistent practice routine. Scheduling specific times for mindful breathing ensures that it becomes an integral part of one's day rather than an afterthought. For example, setting aside five minutes each morning before starting the day can help establish a stable routine. As the practice becomes habitual, the duration or frequency increments can be introduced gradually. This approach helps cultivate mindfulness without overwhelming the individual, creating a sustainable habit that aligns with their lifestyle.

Incorporating breath exercises into regular activities is another effective strategy for habit formation. Associating these practices with daily routines, such as taking deep breaths while waiting for the coffee to brew or performing focused breathing during a commute, can seamlessly integrate mindfulness into various aspects of life. By linking breathing exercises to existing habits, individuals create a natural rhythm that facilitates consistency. Over time, mindful breathing intertwines with everyday actions, reinforcing positive changes without extra effort.

Technology can support regular mindful breathing, especially for beginners needing guidance. Various apps and devices are designed to assist with mindfulness, offering guided breathing exercises, meditation sessions, and progress-tracking features. These tools provide structured support and accountability, helping users stay committed to their practice. For instance, utilizing a smartphone app that sends reminders to take mindful breaks throughout the day can be beneficial in maintaining focus and ensuring regular engagement. Incorporating technology not only aids in establishing a routine but also enhances the overall experience by providing insights and adapting to individual preferences.

While building a mindful breathing practice, it's essential to acknowledge that persistence matters more than perfection. Even brief moments of mindfulness can contribute to long-term benefits, fostering emotional intelligence and resilience against stress. Encouraging a mindset that values small, incremental progress over immediate results can transform obstacles into opportunities for growth. Understanding that practicing mindful breathing doesn't have to be flawless provides the latitude needed to explore different techniques and discover what works best for each person at various journey stages.

Associating mindful breathing with positive experiences amplifies its effectiveness and promotes lasting change. Aligning breathing exercises with pleasurable activities - like listening to soothing music or enjoying nature - can make the practice more appealing and enjoyable. Positive reinforcement motivates, making it easier to maintain a routine even when faced with challenges. The joy derived from these associations creates a feedback loop where mindfulness becomes synonymous with pleasure, encouraging continued participation and deeper exploration into other aspects of personal improvement.

Creating a personalized mindfulness plan that fits your needs and lifestyle is crucial. Mindful breathing should be flexible enough to adapt to changing circumstances while remaining consistent in its foundational purpose. Individuals might begin with simple exercises like inhale counting and gradually incorporate more complex techniques as comfort increases. The ability to customize the practice allows for creativity and adaptability, ensuring it remains relevant and engaging.

Another critical factor is community involvement or social support, which can reinforce the commitment to mindful breathing practices. Engaging with others who share similar goals fosters mutual encouragement and accountability. Through group classes, online communities, or informal gatherings, sharing experiences and insights can deepen understanding and motivation. Social connections also provide diverse perspectives that enrich personal practice, opening new avenues for expanding mindfulness within everyday life.

To maximize the benefits of mindful breathing, cultivating self-compassion and patience is vital. Accepting that each day presents different challenges and opportunities allows individuals to relinquish rigid expectations and embrace imperfection. Viewing setbacks as part of the learning process strengthens resolve and fosters a compassionate attitude towards oneself. Acknowledging that growth comes through experimentation and discovery makes room for ongoing development, turning mindful breathing into a journey rather than a destination.

What small changes can you make today to incorporate mindful breathing into your daily habits, and how might this improve your overall well-being?

Bringing It All Together

This chapter has explored how mindful breathing can effectively calm the mind and reduce anxiety. By focusing on various techniques such as diaphragmatic breathing, box breathing, and the 4-7-8 method, readers have been introduced to accessible methods that enhance mindfulness. These exercises act as anchors, stabilizing us in turbulent times and helping interrupt harmful cycles of stress-inducing thoughts. By recognizing the connection between breath patterns and emotional states, individuals are empowered to understand their reactions better and make conscious adjustments to foster relaxation and clarity.

For those new to these practices, it's encouraging to know mindful breathing doesn't require extensive training or particular environments; it can be seamlessly integrated into daily routines. Whether during a morning ritual or a brief pause at work, these techniques offer a reliable refuge from life's pressures. With patience and consistency, incorporating breathwork can significantly improve mental health and emotional intelligence. Remember, each mindful breath reminds you of your ability to navigate life's challenges with grace and resilience.

How can you commit to practicing mindful breathing regularly, and what benefits do you hope to see as you deepen this practice?

Here is what Megan learned from reading the chapter:

Megan found that this chapter on mindful breathing came at the perfect time in her mindfulness journey. Having already learned about the basics of mindfulness, this chapter offered her practical breathing techniques that she could easily apply to her daily life. For Megan, the simplicity of these exercises stood out. She appreciated how accessible mindful breathing is, especially since it doesn't require special equipment or hours of meditation, just the intention to focus on the breath.

The technique that resonated most with Megan was diaphragmatic breathing. As someone who often experiences anxiety, she noticed how her breath tends to become shallow and rapid during stressful moments. The idea of practicing belly breathing, where she could consciously slow her breath and engage her diaphragm, felt like a tangible way to regain control. She found the instructions easy to follow and started practicing this method during her lunch breaks, feeling more centered afterward. The connection between deep breaths and reduced stress hormones made her even more committed to making this a daily habit.

Megan also appreciated the 4-7-8 breathing technique, which she found helpful before bed. Struggling with restless thoughts at night is something she's been dealing with for a while, and the structured nature of this technique helped her feel more in control of her mind before sleep. By focusing on the inhale-hold-exhale pattern, Megan noticed her thoughts slowing down, and it was easier to transition into a calmer state. She plans to use this technique consistently to improve her sleep quality.

What Megan liked most about this chapter was how it connected to what she had learned about overthinking. In those moments when her mind races with worry or doubt, these mindful breathing techniques provided her with tools to ground herself. By focusing on the rhythm of her breath, she could interrupt those anxious thoughts, reminding herself of the importance of being present. She realized that, like mindfulness, breathing is a way to bring herself back to the moment and away from spiraling thoughts.

Megan's plan moving forward is to continue integrating these breathing techniques into her daily routine. She's already using mindful breathing during work breaks and before bed, but she wants to expand this to other parts of her day, such as during her commute or while waiting in line. Tying these practices to everyday activities made mindfulness feel more natural to her. Megan is excited to see how these small changes in her breath can lead to a greater sense of calm and emotional balance, especially during stressful periods.

Chapter 4: Healing Through Meditation: Breaking Free from Overthinking

Meditation is a powerful tool for calming the constant whirl of overthinking, offering pathways to mental serenity and clarity. Overthinking can spiral into anxiety and stress, overwhelming our ability to enjoy life fully. Here lies the significance of meditation, an adaptable practice capable of taming the tumultuous mind. By focusing inward, meditation offers a sanctuary - a pause amidst life's chaos - to gain insight into our anxious thoughts and learn to release them with compassion. This chapter invites you to journey through diverse meditation practices, each offering a unique approach to managing overthink and attaining peace.

In this exploration, you delve into various meditative styles that can reshape your relationship with your thoughts. You will discover how mindfulness meditation encourages present-moment awareness, helping you detach from habitual rumination patterns. On the other hand, loving-kindness meditation nurtures self-compassion, counteracting negativity with kindness. The chapter also introduces transcendental meditation's calming mantra techniques for more profound relaxation alongside guided meditations that provide structured support that is particularly useful for beginners. As you traverse these methods, you'll be equipped to find a practice that resonates personally with your needs and lifestyle, empowering you to incorporate meditation as a steady ally in your daily routine. In doing so, the goal is not to silence the mind completely but to cultivate a harmonious state where thoughts arise and ebb away effortlessly, allowing you to engage with life more fully and joyfully.

How could incorporating meditation into your daily life help you break free from the cycles of overthinking that affect your peace of mind?

Different Styles of Meditation

Overthinking can be an all-consuming habit, trapping us in cycles of worry and anxiety. Fortunately, meditation offers diverse pathways to break free, each uniquely designed to address different aspects of mental clutter. Let's delve into some styles that introduce tranquility and clarity by helping us manage to overthink.

First, consider mindfulness meditation, which focuses on present-moment awareness. Mindfulness meditation encourages us to observe our thoughts and bodily sensations without judgment. It invites us to pay attention to our breathing, the subtle shifts of energy or the sounds around us, all without trying to change anything. Regular practice helps reduce anxiety by teaching us to live in the moment instead of getting swept away by past or future worries. Research shows it can improve emotional intelligence by enhancing self-awareness and reducing impulsive reactions (Happiness.com, 2021).

Another transformative practice is loving-kindness meditation, or Metta meditation, which focuses on developing compassion toward oneself and others. This approach focuses on developing compassion towards oneself and others. By cultivating goodwill and kindness, you can counteract negative emotions like self-criticism. Try sitting quietly, allowing your breath to guide you as you repeat phrases like "May I be happy" or "May I be safe." Gradually extend these wishes toward loved ones, acquaintances, and even those you find challenging. The process nurtures a sense of empathy and connection, building bridges of understanding across differences (Morales-Brown, 2023).

For those seeking deep relaxation, transcendental meditation (TM) offers an intriguing option. Incorporating a mantra, often a simple sound or word, TM allows practitioners to transcend their current mental state. This repetition calms the mind and leads to a distinctive form of restful alertness. Daily practice can enhance resilience against stress, making it easier to navigate life's challenges with grace and composure. While traditional TM involves a certified instructor assigning a personal mantra, modern approaches allow flexibility in choosing your focal point.

Guided meditation provides a structured entry into meditation, which is particularly beneficial for beginners. Unlike self-guided practices, guided meditation involves following the instructions from an experienced practitioner or a recorded session. These sessions might include themes such as stress relief, gratitude, or self-acceptance. They gently steer your focus, offering prompts to explore specific thoughts or visualize peaceful settings. By providing direction, guided meditations reduce the intimidation factor often associated with starting a new practice, fostering confidence while aiding in developing a consistent habit.

Each meditation style offers unique benefits, and it's crucial to remember that there's no one-size-fits-all approach. Finding the right style may require experimentation, patience, and openness to different experiences. Whether you're drawn to the silent reflection of mindfulness meditation or the comforting embrace of a guided session, the key is cultivating a practice that resonates with you.

Incorporating meditation into daily life can be a manageable task. Start with five minutes daily, gradually increasing the duration as you become more comfortable. Consistency is vital; regular practice can significantly influence mental health, making stressful situations more manageable and promoting mental clarity and balance. Integrating these practices into your routine creates a personalized toolkit for battling overthinking and achieving a greater sense of peace and well-being.

Which meditation style resonates most with your current needs, and how can you explore it to help manage your overthinking more effectively?

Meditation Setup and Environment

Creating a conducive meditation environment is essential for managing overthinking and achieving inner peace. The physical space where you meditate can significantly influence your practice's effectiveness, helping you focus, relax, and maintain consistency. Let's explore how to craft such an environment with supportive elements and tools.

Choosing the right location for your meditation practice is foundational. Ideally, I would like to find a spot that is quiet and free from distractions. This might be a dedicated room, a snug corner of your bedroom, or even a tiny section of your living room. The key is selecting a place that signals your mind to calm down and focus once you step into it. When surrounded by tranquility, you can more easily meditate without battling external noise or interruptions. If privacy is a concern, use a curtain or room divider to create a personal nook separate from daily life (Flynn, 2024).

Once you've chosen your location, enhancing this space with comforting elements can further encourage relaxation. Add cushions or a meditation bench to make sitting more comfortable, allowing you to remain undisturbed for longer sessions. Bringing in aspects of nature can also soothe and ground your space. Place some houseplants or flowers around, adding aesthetic value and fostering a sense of calm and connection to nature. Add soothing scents with candles, incense, or essential oils like lavender or sandalwood.

Lighting also plays a critical role; soft, natural lighting is preferable. If possible, set up near a window that lets in ample daylight. Opt for warm, dimmable lights or candles in the evening to create a tranquil ambiance. Experimenting with lighting can help you tune the environment to one that feels most inviting and peaceful.

Timing is another crucial factor to consider. Establishing a regular meditation routine can significantly aid habit formation and seamlessly integrate your practice into your daily life. Early mornings are recommended as they present fewer distractions and provide a serene start to your day. Alternatively, evenings work better for some, offering a chance to unwind from the day's stresses before bedtime. By meditating at these times, you not only enhance your focus but also create a consistent ritual that becomes second nature.

Various tools can enhance focus and track progress to support your meditation journey, thereby increasing engagement and personalization of your practice. Apps designed for meditation offer guided sessions, ambient soundscapes, and progress-tracking features. This digital assistance can be particularly beneficial for beginners who need guidance or seasoned practitioners looking for variety. A meditation timer can also be handy, allowing you to set session lengths without the distraction of checking a clock, thus maintaining a deeper meditative state.

Personalization is critical to creating a space that resonates with you. Infuse the area with objects that have personal significance or inspire peace and introspection—a cherished piece of artwork, spiritual symbols, or even personal mementos. These items can ground you to the present moment and remind you of your meditation's purpose. Moreover, keep the space tidy and decluttered. An organized environment mirrors a clear mind, enabling you to dive into your practice without unnecessary mental chatter.

How can you create a calming space in your home or routine that supports a consistent and peaceful meditation practice?

Amelie Brooks

Guided vs. Solo Meditation

Overthinking is common in our fast-paced world, but meditation offers a way to break free. Two main types of meditative practices - guided and solo - each have unique advantages and challenges that can be important tools on your journey to finding inner peace.

Guided meditation is like having a map while exploring unfamiliar territory. It typically involves the guidance of an instructor or an audio track designed to lead practitioners through the meditation process. This approach is particularly beneficial for beginners who need to feel confident navigating their meditation practice independently. With guided sessions, you're often led to focus on specific challenges, such as stress relief or insomnia, offering reassurance and clarity. The structure of guided meditation can be comforting, reducing concerns about doing things "right," which can cause anxiety. However, relying too much on external instructions might limit personal exploration and spontaneity.

On the other hand, solo meditation allows for a more personalized and autonomous experience. Meditating alone has no predetermined paths; instead, the practitioner can tailor sessions according to their mood, needs, and goals. This independence fosters self-discipline and the ability to listen to one's intuition. Solo meditation can adapt day-to-day, fluctuating with one's emotional state, providing the flexibility to explore different techniques and approaches instinctively. However, without the framework of an instructor, it may be challenging at first to maintain focus or to know how to handle wandering thoughts. This challenge becomes an opportunity to develop concentration and resilience with time and practice.

Combining guided and solo meditation may offer the best of both worlds, especially for those just starting or looking to deepen their practice. By beginning with guided sessions, individuals can gain foundational skills and confidence. Once familiar with the basics, transitioning gradually into solo meditation can cultivate a stronger sense of mastery and self-reliance. This integration also supports resilience since the combined experience can provide insights into how different methods can address various aspects of life. For instance, during particularly stressful periods, one might revert to guided sessions for comfort while returning to solo practice for daily maintenance and growth. A helpful guideline here is to experiment with integrating one weekend day of solo practice into a routine primarily consisting of guided sessions, allowing a natural progression.

Reflective practices, such as journaling, pair harmoniously with meditation, deepening your understanding and enhancing your mindfulness journey. Journaling bridges your meditative experiences and daily life, offering a space to record insights and track emotional responses over time. Through written reflection, patterns and triggers of overthinking can become more apparent, empowering you to make informed changes. For example, by jotting down thoughts post-meditation, you might notice recurring themes that arise during moments of peace or stress, leading to valuable realizations about what influences your mental chatter. Such reflective practices further enhance emotional intelligence, as they encourage self-awareness and empathy, essential components of personal growth.

Additionally, maintaining a journal can aid in identifying progress and celebrating achievements, which reinforces motivation and commitment. Tracking entries over weeks or months, you'll likely observe shifts in emotional responses and mental reactions, revealing gradual improvements you might otherwise overlook. This documentation serves as a motivational tool and fosters a deeper connection with oneself, nurturing a comforting sense of self-compassion.

How would alternating between guided and solo meditation sessions offer you flexibility and confidence in managing overthinking and emotional stress?

Tracking Progress and Experiences

Tracking your meditation progress can be an essential element in managing overthinking. By monitoring your journey, you gain insights into how each practice affects you, revealing patterns contributing to overthinking. This process empowers you to make more informed decisions about which practices serve your needs best and where adjustments might be necessary. One helpful tool for this exploration is the mindfulness journal.

Mindfulness journals offer a dedicated space for daily reflections and observations. Writing down your thoughts after each session deepens self-awareness and highlights recurring overthinking patterns. For instance, by regularly noting how you feel before and after meditation, you may start identifying triggers or thought patterns that perpetuate anxiety or distress. Over time, these written reflections become a valuable record, enabling you to see tangible progress and make connections between meditation practices and emotional shifts. This enhanced self-awareness is a foundational step toward breaking free from overthinking cycles.

Setting realistic goals is another vital aspect of tracking progress to complement journaling. Establishing achievable milestones fosters a sense of accomplishment and motivation. In meditation, this could mean setting a goal to meditate for five minutes a day for a week and then gradually increasing the duration or frequency. You remain committed without feeling overwhelmed by breaking down larger aspirations into smaller, manageable objectives. These small victories build momentum, reinforcing your resolve and demonstrating that real change occurs incrementally.

Incorporating apps and tools into your routine can add an engaging element to your meditation practice. Many modern apps gamify meditation, offering visual representations of your progress, such as streaks or milestone badges. These features make meditation interactive, enhancing your commitment by providing feedback and a sense of achievement. Visualizing progress in this manner keeps you motivated and reminds you of your dedication to managing overthinking through mindfulness.

The importance of periodic reviews must be balanced. Regularly assessing your journey lets you reflect on emotional changes and celebrate successes, no matter how small. Such reviews provide an opportunity to pause and recognize growth, cultivating gratitude for the ongoing mindfulness journey. During these assessments, ask yourself: How has my ability to stay present evolved? Have I noticed a decreased overthinking or heightened awareness of when it happens? Could you acknowledge these positive changes to reinforce the value of your efforts and maintain enthusiasm?

When integrating these methods, it's important to remember that everyone's journey is unique. What works for one person might not work for another, so it is crucial to tailor your approach based on personal preferences and experiences. Some individuals may greatly benefit from writing detailed entries in their mindfulness journals, while others may prefer brief notes or voice recordings. Similarly, some might thrive using structured meditation apps with specific guided sessions, whereas others might favor a more flexible, intuitive practice. The key lies in experimentation and adaptation, allowing your journey to unfold naturally according to your needs.

It's also beneficial to periodically revisit your initial motivations for meditating. Reflecting on what prompted you to begin the practice can help you, especially during challenging times when progress feels slow. You may have started meditating to reduce stress or seek greater clarity in your thoughts. Whatever the reason, reconnecting with that original intention provides a powerful reminder of why this journey matters, reinforcing your commitment to the path of healing through meditation.

How could journaling about meditation sessions help you identify overthinking patterns and track your emotional growth over time?

Final Insights

In conclusion, exploring these meditation styles offers a valuable toolkit for managing overthinking and nurturing inner peace. Whether you embrace the gentle awareness of mindfulness, the heartwarming connection of loving-kindness, or the deep relaxation of transcendental meditation, each approach can significantly contribute to personal growth. The chapter highlighted how these practices reduce anxiety and improve emotional intelligence by enhancing our capacity for self-awareness and empathy. By experimenting with different techniques, you can find what resonates with you, recognizing there's no single path to tranquility.

In addition to choosing a meditation style, a supportive environment is pivotal in establishing a consistent practice. Transforming a space into a calming retreat—whether through adding nature elements or adjusting lighting, reinforces your commitment to mindfulness. This chapter also underscored the importance of maintaining a journal or using meditation apps to track progress, providing insights into emotional shifts and helping identify triggers of overthinking. With patience and consistency, integrating these practices into your daily routine becomes more intuitive, allowing you to harness the power of mindfulness. Embrace the journey with an open heart, knowing each step is meaningful toward a balanced and peaceful mind.

What small steps can you take today to commit to a meditation practice that nurtures inner peace and reduces overthinking?

Here is what Megan learned from reading the chapter:

Megan found this chapter on meditation deeply insightful, as it tied together much of what she had already explored about mindfulness and overthinking. The idea that meditation could provide a structured way to calm her mind and break free from repetitive, anxious thoughts resonated with her. Having previously struggled with overthinking, she appreciated the variety of meditation styles offered, allowing her to experiment and find a practice that suited her current needs.

Mindfulness meditation was particularly appealing to Megan. She had already dabbled in mindfulness techniques from previous chapters, so this meditation felt like a natural extension. The focus on observing thoughts without judgment aligned perfectly with her ongoing goal of detaching from overthinking. Megan could see how practicing mindfulness meditation regularly might help her stay more present and not get caught up in anxious predictions or regrets about the past.

Loving-kindness meditation was another technique that piqued Megan's interest, especially since she often struggled with self-criticism. The idea of actively cultivating compassion toward herself and others through simple phrases like "May I be happy" felt empowering. Megan could imagine how repeating these mantras might help soften harsh judgments she often places on herself, creating a more compassionate inner dialogue.

The chapter's exploration of guided versus solo meditation gave Megan valuable insight. She realized that starting with guided meditation might give her the structure and support she needs as a beginner. Still, she was intrigued by the idea of eventually transitioning to solo practice to develop more self-reliance.

Journaling after her sessions, as suggested in the chapter, felt like a meaningful way to track her progress and better understand her overthinking patterns. Megan liked the idea of reflecting on her meditation sessions to gain insight into her triggers and celebrate minor improvements along the way.

What stood out most to Megan was how meditation could be adaptable and personal. She appreciated the encouragement to experiment with different styles and techniques without feeling pressured to follow a rigid path. Much like her journey with mindfulness and breathing exercises, meditation felt like another tool she could integrate into her routine, providing flexibility depending on her emotional state and needs.

In the future, Megan plans to start small by incorporating five minutes of guided meditation into her mornings, creating a peaceful transition into the day. As she becomes more comfortable with meditation, she hopes to explore different techniques, eventually building the confidence to practice solo. The chapter reinforced that consistency was critical, but Megan felt reassured knowing she could tailor her practice to fit her lifestyle. Meditation became a steady ally in managing her overthinking and achieving greater mental clarity.

Chapter 5: Emotion Regulation through Mindfulness

Emotion regulation through mindfulness involves embracing self-awareness and understanding to manage our emotions better. In the whirlwind of daily life, our feelings can feel like an untamed storm, leaving us overwhelmed and anxious. Yet, by harnessing mindfulness, you can learn to navigate these emotional waters with grace and calm. Mindfulness allows us to observe our feelings without judgment, giving us the space to respond rather than react impulsively. It helps create a buffer between our emotions and actions, offering a sense of control and peace in moments that might otherwise lead to turmoil.

In this chapter, you delve into various techniques to enhance emotional regulation through mindfulness. The journey begins with gaining awareness and identifying our emotions, understanding your feelings and why. You then explore the art of mindful pauses, learning to take a step back before responding, which can transform our interactions and improve our relationships. Additionally, the chapter introduces grounding methods for diffusing negative emotions, providing practical exercises that anchor us in the present moment. These strategies are essential tools for enhancing personal resilience and fostering emotional intelligence. By implementing these practices, readers will discover accessible ways to fortify their emotional well-being and apply these insights to cope more effectively with life's challenges.

How could mindfulness help you create more space between your emotions and reactions, allowing for greater control in challenging moments?

Identifying and Naming Emotions

Understanding and regulating emotions can seem daunting, especially when life feels overwhelming. However, the journey to emotional regulation begins with a simple yet powerful step: awareness. Becoming more attuned to your emotions lays the foundation for healthier emotional management strategies. Emotional awareness allows us to pause, reflect, and respond constructively to our feelings.

Expanding our emotional vocabulary is one of the first steps to enhancing emotional awareness. Accurately describing your feelings significantly influences how you understand and manage them. Research by Vine et al. (2020) suggests that rich emotional vocabularies are linked to better mental and physical health. Recognizing the difference between feeling "anxious," "nervous," or "excited" can provide insight into the underlying causes, allowing you to address them more effectively. Expanding your emotional vocabulary involves learning precise words to express complex feelings and using them regularly. This practice can help individuals communicate more effectively with themselves and others, leading to deeper emotional understanding and well-being.

Awareness plays a crucial role in helping us process emotions rather than allowing them to become overwhelming. When you maintain an understanding of our emotional states, you acknowledge their presence and permit yourself to feel without judgment. This acknowledgment can prevent emotions from building up and manifesting in unmanageable ways. By being mindful, you can observe emotions, understand their origins, and decide whether they serve you or if you need to adjust your perspectives. This cautious approach prevents us from reacting impulsively or getting swept away by intense feelings.

To further enhance emotional awareness, journaling can be an excellent tool. Journaling prompts encourage introspection and help clarify your thoughts and feelings. Regularly writing about your emotions can reveal patterns in how you respond to specific situations, enabling you to predict better and manage future reactions. For instance, starting a journal entry with prompts such as "What am I feeling right now?" or "What happened today that triggered this emotion?" can uncover recurring themes in your emotional landscape. Over time, journaling becomes a space for emotional exploration and a record that highlights your growth and resilience in handling emotions.

Moreover, examining case studies of individuals who have honed their emotional identification skills can be incredibly inspiring. These narratives demonstrate that understanding emotions isn't just transformative on a personal level but can also positively impact interpersonal relationships and overall life satisfaction. Consider the example of a young professional who initially struggled to identify her anxiety amidst workplace stress. By working with a therapist, she learned to articulate her emotions using a broader vocabulary and employed journaling techniques to reflect on her daily experiences. Her heightened awareness allowed her to manage stress more effectively, improving job performance and personal contentment.

Such stories underscore the potential of emotional awareness as a powerful tool for personal transformation. Sharing these stories illustrates that anyone, regardless of their starting point, can learn to navigate their emotional terrain more skillfully. Moreover, seeing tangible success through others' experiences often reinforces motivation to pursue similar paths in one's own life.

How accurately do you identify and name your emotions, and how might expanding your emotional vocabulary help you better understand and manage your feelings?

Mindful Pauses Before Responding

Pausing before reacting is fundamental to gaining emotional control and enhancing well-being. Introducing mindful pauses can be transformative in our fast-paced world, where immediate reactions are often the norm. These pauses act as brief moments to recalibrate and choose how you wish to respond rather than falling prey to impulsive reactions.

Mindful pauses are intentional breaks that allow you to observe your emotions and thoughts before acting. They help reduce impulsivity driven by strong emotions like anger or frustration. For instance, could you imagine receiving an upsetting email at work? An immediate reaction might lead to writing a hasty reply filled with emotional outbursts. However, taking a moment to pause can prevent potential misunderstandings and regrets. This pause helps calm the immediate surge of emotion, allowing for more thoughtful and constructive responses.

Establishing pauses can be facilitated by several techniques, the most prominent being deep breathing. Deep breathing is a physical cue to signal to the body and mind that it's time to slow down. It involves inhaling deeply through the nose, holding the breath for a few seconds, and exhaling slowly through the mouth. This simple yet effective technique can be practiced anywhere, giving you a quick method to center yourself. Alongside deep breathing, another helpful technique is counting to ten before responding. It creates a buffer zone that allows individuals to detach temporarily from the triggering stimulus, granting them space to think clearly.

During these pauses, engaging in self-reflection is crucial. This involves assessing the situation and one's emotional state with a strategic mindset. Asking questions like, "Why am I feeling this way?" or "What is the best way to address this situation?" can provide clarity and insight. Such reflection encourages a deeper understanding of personal triggers and emotional patterns, paving the way for improved emotional intelligence. Examining our feelings during these moments creates opportunities for growth and self-awareness.

Moreover, mindful pauses have profound implications for communication and relationship quality. When you pause, it allows us to listen more attentively and respond with greater empathy. This approach fosters open dialogue and mutual understanding. Instead of reacting defensively or aggressively, a well-timed pause can prevent escalation and miscommunication. For example, suppose a friend makes an offhand comment that feels hurtful instead of snapping back thoughtlessly. In that case, pausing enables one to consider possible intentions behind the words and respond with kindness or seek clarification.

Research supports the notion that integrating pauses into daily interactions enhances interpersonal relations. By choosing our responses carefully, you engage in healthier, more meaningful exchanges, strengthening bonds and better collaboration. This is especially relevant in professional settings where teamwork and clear communication are vital.

While the benefits of mindful pauses are evident, incorporating them into daily life requires conscious effort and practice. Initially, it may feel unnatural to interrupt automatic response patterns. A practical guideline for developing this habit is to attach the practice of pausing to routine activities, such as waiting at traffic lights or standing in line. Using these mundane moments to practice deep breathing or reflection can strengthen the neural pathways associated with mindful pausing, making it easier to implement in emotionally charged situations.

Additionally, setting reminders throughout the day or using apps designed for mindfulness can help cultivate a consistent practice. Over time, what starts as a deliberate effort can transform into a natural component of one's emotional toolkit.

By mastering the art of pausing, individuals gain better control over their emotional landscape and contribute positively to their social environments. The ability to stop, evaluate, and proceed consciously unlocks the potential for more harmonious and fulfilling interactions.

How often do you pause before reacting to strong emotions, and how could practicing mindful pauses improve your interactions and emotional well-being?

Techniques to Diffuse Negative Feelings

Grounding techniques are critical for effectively managing and diffusing negative emotions. These exercises are designed to anchor individuals in the present moment, helping them escape spirals of negative thinking that often exacerbate feelings of anxiety or distress. A popular method is the 5-4-3-2-1 technique, which utilizes the five senses. By identifying five things you can see, four you can touch, three sounds you can hear, two scents you can smell, and one taste you can locate, you reorient yourself to your immediate environment. This simple yet powerful exercise helps draw attention from overwhelming emotions to a more stable reality.

A step-by-step guide could also be helpful here for you. Begin by placing your feet firmly on the ground, feeling its solidity beneath you. Take slow, deep breaths, each inhale and exhale, grounding you further in the present. As you breathe, observe your surroundings. Look for details you might ordinarily miss, such as the texture of the walls or the play of light across a surface. For added effect, say out loud what you notice about your current environment; this verbalization reinforces the sense of being grounded in the now.

Emotional validation is another essential technique for managing negative emotions. Validating one's feelings means acknowledging and accepting them without judgment. People who experience intense emotions often feel pressured to dismiss or suppress these feelings. Still, validation provides the space to recognize that these emotions, although unpleasant, are reasonable and understandable responses to specific events. These negative emotions naturally diminish in intensity, allowing you to feel without resistance. When a person acknowledges their feelings, it can reduce the internal conflict and self-criticism that exacerbate emotional distress.

Visualization exercises provide a guided escape from taxing emotional states. These techniques allow individuals to mentally transport themselves to calming places or imagine scenarios that induce peace and relaxation. One effective visualization involves picturing a serene location, a forest clearing bathed in sunlight, waves gently rolling onto a quiet beach, or a cozy room filled with soft light. In this mental space, visualize yourself engaging all your senses: the sound of rustling leaves or crashing waves, warm sunlight on your skin, or the scent of ocean air. This total sensory immersion can provide temporary respite from negative emotions, offering a brief interlude of calm and clarity amidst chaos.

Much like visualization, cognitive restructuring shifts negative thought patterns by reframing experiences in a more positive light. This technique, rooted in cognitive behavioral therapy, encourages individuals to critically evaluate their thoughts and challenge inaccuracies or distortions. By examining evidence that supports or contradicts negative thoughts, people can view their experiences through a lens of realism rather than negativity. A practical approach is the Fact Checking Thoughts Worksheet, which prompts individuals to assess whether their thoughts are based on facts or assumptions. Engaging in this process regularly can cultivate optimism, transforming automatic adverse reactions into more constructive and balanced responses. The goal is not to deny challenges but to reframe them as surmountable, fostering resilience and positive outlooks.

These methods serve as valuable tools for anyone seeking to manage their emotions mindfully. Grounding techniques bring clarity and presence, while emotional validation fosters acceptance and understanding. Visualization exercises offer an imaginative escape, promoting relaxation and peace, whereas cognitive restructuring empowers individuals to reshape their mindset towards positivity and resilience. These strategies enable individuals to navigate their emotional landscapes more efficiently, enhancing their overall emotional well-being.

Admittedly, integrating these techniques into daily life requires practice and commitment. It might seem challenging to remember to employ these methods in moments of heightened emotion. However, they become inherent parts of one's coping repertoire over time. Start small by choosing one technique to incorporate into your routine. Perhaps begin with grounding exercises during breakfast or cognitive restructuring at the end of the day to reflect on any particularly challenging thoughts or events.

Also, could you consider using reminders or triggers throughout the day? Simple cues like stickers on mirrors, alarms on phones, or notes in visible places can prompt action when needed most. Sharing these techniques with friends or support groups can reinforce their applicability and offer shared learning opportunities. Incorporating mindfulness into daily life can transform fleeting experiments into enduring habits, significantly improving emotional health.

Which grounding or cognitive techniques could you integrate into your daily routine to help manage and diffuse negative emotions more effectively?

Building Emotional Resilience

Emotional resilience is fundamental to well-being and mental health. It represents our capacity to adapt, recover, and thrive in the face of stress and adversity. For many grappling with anxiety, understanding resilience opens avenues for personal growth and empowerment. Resilience isn't about avoiding difficulties but confronting challenges and emerging stronger. As noted by experts, this ability to bounce back stems from learning healthy coping mechanisms and drawing upon community resources (National Institutes of Health, 2022). Mindfulness practices can bolster this trait, nurturing your emotional well-being.

Mindfulness, inherently grounded in present-moment awareness, offers practical strategies to promote resilience and stabilize emotional responses. Imagine starting your day with a mindful exercise like deep breathing or a short meditation session. By focusing your attention on your breath, you cultivate a sense of calm that counteracts the chaos of external stressors. Mindful eating or taking deliberate walks - where you attune yourself to each sensation - can transform mundane activities into moments of reflection and tranquility. Such routines provide immediate relief and build a bank of emotional reserves you can draw upon when faced with future stress. Integrating these practices allows you to develop a steady emotional response pattern that grants clarity even amidst turmoil.

Building a robust support network is another cornerstone of emotional resilience. When life's burdens feel overwhelming, having a circle of positive and supportive individuals to turn to can make all the difference. This community provides a safety net that nurtures and encourages, allowing for emotional release and mutual support. To create such networks, actively contact friends, family, or community groups. Shared activities, whether a book club or volunteering for local causes, can help cement these bonds. Identify key supporters in different areas of your life - at work, home, or within your neighborhood - and don't hesitate to lean on them during tough times. Honest communication and conflict resolution skills are vital here, ensuring that relationships remain strong and beneficial.

Setting goals is pivotal for intentional emotional growth and confidence building. You can start by identifying what you want to achieve, whether mastering a new skill, improving your mental health, or enhancing a personal relationship. Clearly defined goals provide a sense of purpose and direction. It would be best to reflect regularly on your progress toward these aims. Celebrate small victories along the way, as these affirmations boost your confidence and motivate continued effort. These reflections also help you learn from setbacks, offering insights that foster resilience and adaptability. Remember, goal setting is not a rigid process; it's about being flexible and adjusting objectives to match your evolving aspirations and circumstances.

Fostering a sense of gratitude also enhances resilience. By acknowledging things you appreciate daily, you shift focus from negative to positive experiences. This adjustment can be transformative, helping to reframe how you perceive stressful situations. Over time, appreciating life's little joys cultivates a sense of contentment, reinforcing your ability to withstand adversity. Keeping a gratitude journal where you jot down what brings happiness and satisfaction can be a powerful tool for maintaining perspective during challenging times.

In the same vein, self-compassion plays a critical role in emotional resilience. It involves treating yourself with kindness, especially when experiencing difficulty or failure. Instead of harsh self-criticism, practice gentle understanding. Remind yourself that making mistakes is a natural part of learning. This shift in mindset reduces self-imposed stress and fosters a healthier, more balanced emotional outlook.

While resilience can often feel like an individual journey, remember that its foundation is deeply rooted in collective experiences and community connections; engage in activities that strengthen your ties with others, share your experiences, and be open to learning from theirs. This builds your resilience and contributes to the strength of those around you, creating a ripple effect that benefits entire communities.

What steps can you take to build emotional resilience, and how can mindfulness practices like meditation and self-compassion contribute to this growth?

Wrapping Up

As we've journeyed through this chapter, the significance of developing mindful emotional management skills and their impact on our well-being has become evident. By naming and understanding our emotions, expanding our emotional vocabulary, and pausing mindfully before responding, you lay the groundwork for healthier relationships and more balanced lives. These practices empower us to navigate our emotional landscapes with more excellent skill, offering opportunities for personal growth and deeper connections with others.

These techniques are transformative for those frequently overwhelmed by anxiety or seeking personal growth. Incorporating practices such as journaling, grounding exercises, and visualization can enrich your emotional resilience toolkit. Remember, the path to enhanced emotional intelligence is a personal endeavor that requires patience and practice. Through consistent training and reflection, you build a more resilient self, capable of facing life's challenges with empathy and strength.

How can you commit to consistently using mindfulness techniques to improve your emotional regulation and strengthen your relationships with others?

Here is what Megan learned from reading the chapter:

Megan found this chapter on emotion regulation through mindfulness particularly valuable, as it helped her understand how to manage her emotions more intentionally and compassionately. She realized how often she reacts impulsively when overwhelmed by anxiety, and the idea of creating space between her feelings and reactions resonated deeply with her. By using mindfulness techniques, she could see how this would give her the clarity to respond thoughtfully instead of reacting out of frustration or fear.

One of Megan's key takeaways was identifying and naming her emotions more accurately. She often feels a rush of emotions but struggles to pinpoint her feelings. The suggestion to expand her emotional vocabulary seemed like a practical step. Megan realized that by better understanding whether she's feeling "anxious," "frustrated," or "overwhelmed," she could start to address the root cause of her feelings more effectively. This awareness, combined with mindfulness, could help her approach her emotions with more self-compassion.

The chapter's focus on mindful pauses before reacting also stood out to Megan. She often feels rushed into making decisions or responding when emotions are high, especially at work. Taking a deep breath or counting to ten before reacting felt like a manageable way to bring mindfulness into her daily interactions. Megan could see how this practice would improve her emotional regulation and enhance her relationships by allowing her to respond with more empathy and patience.

Like the 5-4-3-2-1 method, Grounding techniques were another tool Megan found appealing. Since she often feels overwhelmed by negative thoughts, especially during stressful times, using her senses to ground herself in the present moment felt empowering. Megan could see how these techniques might help her diffuse the intensity of her emotions and bring her back to a calmer state more quickly. She's already considering integrating these grounding exercises into her daily routine, especially when she feels emotionally flooded.

Lastly, the chapter's exploration of building emotional resilience through mindfulness struck a chord with Megan. She has been working on cultivating more self-compassion, and this chapter reinforced the idea that treating herself with kindness during difficult moments would help her develop resilience. Focusing on setting small goals, practicing gratitude, and creating a support network made her feel more optimistic about building a stronger emotional foundation.

Moving forward, Megan plans to integrate these mindfulness techniques into her life more consistently. She will start by expanding her emotional vocabulary, practicing mindful pauses, and using grounding techniques when negative emotions arise. Over time, she hopes these practices will help her manage her feelings, strengthen her relationships, and increase her emotional resilience.

Chapter 6: Body Scan Meditation: Bridging Mind and Body

Body scan meditation connects you with your physical presence, allowing you to explore sensations and tensions within your body. It offers a path to relaxation and emotional awareness by inviting practitioners to journey through each area of the body, unlocking a deeper understanding of themselves. This exploration encourages you to notice subtle cues often overlooked in the hustle of everyday life. This simple yet powerful exercise holds the potential for profound personal growth by cultivating mindfulness through an intimate mind-body connection. The allure of body scanning is found in its accessibility, making it a versatile tool for anyone seeking tranquility amidst life's stresses.

In this chapter, you will delve into the transformative effects of body scan meditation, highlighting how it enhances self-awareness and fosters emotional intelligence. You will discover this practice's simplicity and universal appeal, which requires no prior experience or special equipment. We'll guide you through the steps to create a conducive environment for meditation, allowing you to engage with your internal landscape fully. Additionally, the chapter explores the historical roots of body scans and their integration into modern mindfulness practices, underscoring their enduring relevance in promoting mental and physical well-being. Through this exploration, you'll gain insights into the mechanics and benefits of regular practice, revealing how body scans can become a cornerstone of your wellness routine.

How can body scan meditation help you build a stronger connection between your physical sensations and emotional awareness?

Introduction to Body Scanning

Body scan meditation is a cornerstone of mindfulness, offering individuals a straightforward yet profound way to connect with their physical and emotional selves. It involves consciously directing attention through each body part, identifying sensations or tensions that might go unnoticed. This deliberate awareness allows practitioners to forge a deeper connection with their bodies, making them more attuned to the subtle cues and signals that often get lost in the shuffle of daily life.

Rooted deeply in ancient meditation practices, body scans have transcended time and geography to find a place in modern mindfulness programs across the globe. This integration reflects a broader understanding of how universal and effective these awareness techniques can be. Spanning cultures and centuries, body scans underscore the timeless human need for self-awareness practices that promote mental and physical health.

One of the most appealing aspects of the body scan is its inherent simplicity and accessibility. Unlike other forms of meditation that may require specific skills or environments, a body scan can be done almost anywhere without prior experience. Guided meditations are widely available online or through apps, providing easy access to beginners. This universality means people from all walks of life can benefit from body scanning, whether seated at a desk, lying in bed, or waiting in line. The practice requires no special equipment or knowledge, only an open mind and a willingness to explore your internal landscape.

Beyond relaxation, body scans offer substantial benefits for emotional awareness. While the initial draw might be the promise of stress relief, regular practice can lead to a richer understanding of one's emotions. For instance, recognizing how specific thoughts affect physical tension can offer insights into unresolved issues or stressors. Over time, this enhanced self-awareness fosters a more profound emotional intelligence, enabling individuals to manage stressors with a more straightforward, calmer demeanor.

Delving into the mechanics of a body scan reveals why it's so uniquely powerful. The process starts by focusing on the breath and gradually moving attention through the body. This shift from external to internal awareness encourages practitioners to notice sensations they might typically ignore, such as warmth, tingling, or tension, in various parts of the body. With practice, individuals become more adept at observing these sensations without judgment, cultivating a neutral stance that helps reduce negative self-talk and promotes overall well-being.

Body scan meditation is especially beneficial for those struggling with anxiety or overwhelming thoughts. By anchoring the mind in the present and redirecting focus to bodily sensations, it provides a refuge from the relentless chatter of worries and fears. Doing so allows for moments of peace and clarity, essential components in managing mental health effectively. Individuals who engage regularly with body scans often report an increased ability to cope with daily stresses, attributing this resilience to the practice's grounding effects.

Moreover, the historical context of body scanning enriches its appeal. Understanding that these practices have been utilized for centuries enhances their credibility and allure. Many long-standing traditions, such as yoga and Buddhism, incorporate similar methods to promote self-inquiry and mindfulness, reinforcing the notion that engaging with our inner selves is vital for holistic well-being. Such continuity across time highlights the enduring importance of self-awareness and depicts body scans as a viable tool for achieving it.

The popularity and accessibility of body scans today also play a crucial role in their integration into personal wellness routines. With all its conveniences, modern life comes with challenges, such as overstimulation and constant connectivity. Here, body scans serve as an antidote, providing a simple yet effective method for disconnecting from external distractions and reconnecting with oneself. The proliferation of resources - from guided recordings to mindfulness workshops - ensures that anyone interested can easily access and learn this practice, further solidifying its place in contemporary mindfulness strategies.

For those new to mindfulness, it's crucial to communicate that body scans extend beyond mere relaxation; they foster emotional exploration. This understanding can significantly improve commitment to the practice, as it becomes clear that the benefits extend into areas like empathy, compassion, and emotional regulation. Engaging in body scans can illuminate emotional responses tied to specific physical sensations, shedding light on how unresolved emotions manifest physically. This introspective journey often paves the way for healing, allowing individuals to address underlying issues head-on with newfound insight.

How might becoming more mindful of the physical sensations in your body reveal hidden sources of stress or emotional tension?

Steps to Conduct a Body Scan

To fully benefit from a body scan meditation, setting the stage with intention and care is essential. Setting the stage with intention and care - including creating a conducive environment - plays a significant role in the quality of your practice. Finding a quiet, comfortable space enhances relaxation and minimizes distractions, allowing you to focus solely on the sensations within your body. This preparation is crucial, as it sets the tone for meaningful engagement with the practice. A tranquil setting might be your bedroom, a quiet corner of your living room, or a peaceful spot outdoors surrounded by nature. Ensure the temperature is comfortable, the lighting is soft, and you're positioned lying down or seated with supportive cushions if needed. Creating a comforting environment makes you more likely to achieve a deeper state of relaxation and mindfulness.

Once your surroundings are set, it's time to engage in the body scan itself. For beginners, following a structured step-by-step approach can help demystify the process and instill confidence. Begin at your toes, slowly directing your attention over each part of your body as you move upward to your head. As the focus shifts from one area to the next, take note of any sensations that arise. Warmth, tingling, tension, or ease. Engaging in this sequence, from toes to head, simplifies the body scan, making it approachable even for those new to meditation. This guided journey through your body fosters an awareness that promotes mindfulness, encouraging a meditative state where thoughts can be observed rather than followed.

One of the core aspects of a successful body scan is the practice of non-judgmental observation. As you progress through different parts of your body, observing any sensations without attaching labels or judgments is essential. Avoid critiquing yourself or your reactions if certain areas feel tense or uncomfortable. If you could, gently acknowledge these feelings before moving on. This compassionate approach helps cultivate a healthier relationship with your body by counteracting negative language and encouraging body positivity. Over time, you may notice increased compassion towards yourself as you learn to accept various physical experiences as they are rather than what you think they should be.

Incorporating breathing techniques into your body scan can significantly deepen your practice. Breathing is a natural anchor, grounding you in the present moment and enhancing concentration. As you focus on different body parts, synchronize your breaths to facilitate relaxation. Consider adopting a pattern where you inhale deeply through your nose, hold briefly, and exhale slowly through your mouth. The prolonged exhalation has a calming effect, reinforcing a sense of peace and stillness. This breathing rhythm (inhale for two seconds, hold for one, exhale for four) assists in bringing your attention back whenever it wanders, cultivating a mindful presence throughout the session (Mindfulness and Breathing Techniques for Exam Stress, n.d.).

The beauty of the body scan lies in its adaptability. Whether practiced in the morning to start the day with clarity or in the evening to unwind from the hustle of daily life, it offers a versatile tool for managing stress and fostering overall well-being. Integrating this practice into your routine can lead to profound shifts in how you interact with your body and your broader mindset. With consistency, the discipline of regular scans develops an enhanced sense of bodily and emotional awareness, promoting tranquility and resilience.

What steps can you take to create a calm environment and fully engage in body scan meditation, making it a regular part of your self-care routine?

Noting Sensations and Responses

Body scan meditation can be a rewarding journey into the nuances of self-awareness and relaxation. By encouraging readers to interact thoughtfully with their physical sensations and emotional responses during the process, you can facilitate a more profound connection between mind and body.

A key aspect of body scan meditation is learning to identify and distinguish various sensations within your body. This recognition fosters curiosity and encourages a deepened interaction with the physical self. Often, people may overlook subtle feelings or dismiss them as insignificant, but these sensations can provide valuable insights into our well-being. For instance, tingling, warmth, or tension might reveal areas of stress or discomfort that you unconsciously carry. By tuning into these signals, you can explore your body, unraveling layers of tension or unnoticed stress.

Recognizing emotional responses tied to specific body parts can illuminate paths toward healing underlying emotional issues related to physical tension. Emotions often manifest in the body, with anxiety causing tight shoulders or sadness leading to a heavy chest. By identifying these links during a body scan, individuals can explore the root causes of their physical discomforts. This awareness opens the door to addressing not just the physical manifestations but also the emotional roots. If a knot in the stomach consistently arises when facing specific thoughts, it could suggest more profound emotional work related to fear or anxiety. Such realizations are invaluable for potential pathways to emotional healing and improved mental health.

Practicing non-reactive awareness during body scans cultivates a neutral relationship with bodily sensations. Instead of interpreting pain or discomfort negatively, individuals learn to acknowledge these sensations without judgment. This approach reduces the stress response inherent in negative interpretations, allowing you to practice simple awareness. For example, instead of reacting with frustration to a persistent ache, one learns to observe it calmly, diminishing its power over one's emotions. This practice lessens immediate stress reactions and reinforces a long-term mindset of acceptance and neutrality towards bodily experiences.

Encouraging journaling after the body scan can further reinforce the practice by enabling a continuous dialogue with one's body.

Writing down sensations and emotions noticed during the scan serves as a record that can uncover patterns over time. Journaling prompts reflection and supports the retention of insights gained during each session. By committing these experiences to paper, practitioners solidify their self-awareness and enhance their ongoing engagement with the practice. Furthermore, journaling helps track progress, revealing growth in emotional intelligence and coping mechanisms. Over time, this habit becomes a personal record of transformation, showcasing the positive changes facilitated by regular body scan meditation.

As individuals delve into distinguishing sensations, they embark on a path that encourages open exploration and consideration of the body's language. The initial curiosity leads to greater self-discovery, promoting a healthier relationship with one's physical existence. This process is akin to learning a new language, where each sensation holds unique messages about our condition and needs.

Acknowledging emotional associations with specific body parts provides another layer of understanding. When expressed physically, emotions offer clues to internal conflicts and unresolved issues. With consistent practice, individuals become adept at recognizing these cues, demystifying the complex interplay between mind and body. This recognition can be empowering, clarifying how emotional wellness impacts physical health and vice versa.

Cultivating non-reactive awareness should be seen as liberating, freeing individuals from the tyranny of automatic stress reactions. By fostering a mindset that observes rather than judges, practitioners experience a shift in their relationship with pain. Viewing it not as an adversary but as a teacher. This nuanced perspective encourages peace with one's body, reducing the burden of stress and enhancing overall well-being.

Journaling companions the meditative process, bridging the gap between fleeting perception and lasting insight. As practitioners develop a habit of documenting their experiences, they create a tapestry of personal growth and understanding that informs future sessions. These reflections nurture a dynamic relationship with oneself, emphasizing continuity and commitment to personal evolution through mindful practices.

How can recognizing the physical manifestations of your emotions during a body scan help you better understand and manage your emotional well-being?

Benefits of Regular Practice

Regular body scans in your daily routine can transform your mindfulness and overall well-being. Imagine starting each day with a moment dedicated entirely to tuning in with your own body, fostering a profound awareness that most people overlook amidst the hustle and bustle of daily life. This practice grounds you in the present and helps you develop thoughtful responses to the world around you.

Regular body scans help lessen the burden of overthinking by shifting your focus from constant mental chatter to the subtle sensations of your body. This shift enables you to cultivate a clearer mind, reduce anxiety, and respond thoughtfully to challenges instead of impulsively. For instance, as you begin noticing how stress manifests physically - like tension in your shoulders or tightness in your chest - you learn to acknowledge these feelings without judgment. This heightened awareness fosters a deeper connection to yourself, gradually alleviating the cycle of anxiety and stress.

Moreover, consistent body scanning acts as an effective tool for stress relief. It offers physical benefits such as improved relaxation and resilience against mental health issues like anxiety and depression. Picture it as a mini-vacation for the mind, where noticing each muscle and sensation allows your body to unwind. This improves your overall mental health, making you more resilient and better equipped to handle life's challenges.

Enhanced emotional regulation is another significant benefit of regular body scans. As you become more aware of your emotions through this practice, you develop the ability to manage them more proactively. This improved emotional intelligence translates into better interpersonal relationships. When you understand your feelings better, you interact with others more empathetically and effectively. Consider the situation where you're in a heated argument; recognizing your rising frustration during a scan can empower you to pause, breathe, and choose a calmer response, leading to healthier communication and stronger relationships.

The journey through body scanning often unlocks deeper personal insights regarding one's mental and emotional state. Over time, you may find yourself unearthing patterns or triggers previously buried beneath layers of subconscious habits. This newfound clarity encourages sustained commitment to the practice, leading to a more meaningful dialogue with oneself. For example, realizing that specific thoughts consistently trigger anxiety may motivate you to address those root causes, leading to personal growth.

As you delve deeper into this practice, the cumulative effects are far-reaching. What begins as a few minutes of focused attention on bodily sensations can evolve into a lifelong habit of mindful living. Many practitioners report feeling more aligned with their sense of self, experiencing an overarching calmness that impacts every aspect of their lives. This simple yet profound ritual becomes a cornerstone of their daily existence, helping weave mindfulness seamlessly into the fabric of everyday life.

While incorporating body scans into your routine might require perseverance, especially at the onset, the rewards are immense and far-reaching. Enhanced awareness and relaxation are just the beginning. With patience, you'll likely discover how this practice enriches your interactions, providing tools to navigate life's emotional ebbs and flows better.

What benefits do you hope to gain from incorporating body scan meditation into your daily routine, and how can it help you manage overthinking and stress?

Bringing It All Together

In exploring the practice of body scans, we've ventured into a method that offers profound benefits for both awareness and relaxation. Individuals can cultivate a deeper understanding of themselves by focusing on bodily sensations, revealing tensions and emotions they may typically overlook. This chapter has illuminated how simple yet powerful this practice is, providing a gentle guide for those seeking to manage stress better and enhance their emotional intelligence. For adults and young adults grappling with anxiety or overwhelming thoughts, body scan meditations serve as a valuable resource for grounding and clarity.

As you close this chapter, I'd like you to consider how integrating body scans into your daily routine can transform your approach to mental well-being. They offer a path to relaxation and a doorway to personal growth and healing. Whether new to mindfulness practices or deepening an existing journey, these techniques invite you to connect more meaningfully with yourself. By embracing your body's subtle messages, you gain tools to navigate life's challenges with composure and insight, fostering balance and resilience.

How will you commit to using body scan meditation as a tool to enhance your self-awareness, manage stress, and foster emotional growth?

Here is what Megan learned from reading the chapter:

Megan found this chapter on body scan meditation particularly enlightening, as it opened up a new perspective on how mindfulness could connect her mental and physical well-being. She realized how often she ignores the signals her body is sending, mainly when stress builds up. The idea of consciously tuning into each part of her body felt like a powerful way to bridge the gap between her emotional state and the physical manifestations of that stress.

What stood out most to Megan was how body scan meditation could help her identify hidden sources of tension. She often experiences tightness in her shoulders or a knot in her stomach without fully understanding why. The chapter's emphasis on recognizing these sensations without judgment felt liberating to her, as it aligned with her broader goal of practicing self-compassion. By engaging in regular body scans, Megan could see herself becoming more aware of how her emotions show up physically, which might lead to uncovering and addressing unresolved stressors.

The chapter's step-by-step guide for conducting a body scan benefited Megan, as she felt slightly intimidated by the idea of meditation. Starting with her toes and moving up to her head seemed like a simple and approachable way to ease into the practice. Megan appreciated that there were no strict rules, just a gentle invitation to explore her body's sensations. Incorporating breathing techniques into the process also made sense to her, adding a calming rhythm to the practice and helping her stay grounded when her mind wandered.

Megan also resonated with using body scan meditation to manage overthinking. Since she often struggles with racing thoughts, the practice offered her a way to shift focus from her mind to her body, providing relief from the constant mental chatter. She liked using body scans to ground herself, especially during stressful work or personal moments. The fact that it could be done almost anywhere made it accessible and easy to integrate into her routine.

The concept of non-reactive awareness also felt empowering for Megan. She realized that she could break the cycle of negative self-talk by observing physical sensations without judgment. Megan could see how this practice might help her foster a more neutral relationship with her body, learning to accept discomfort or tension without the added layer of frustration or criticism. This mindset shift seemed like a valuable tool for her emotional growth.

Moving forward, Megan plans to incorporate body scan meditation into her morning routine to set a calming tone for the day. She hopes this practice will help her manage stress and deepen her self-awareness and emotional intelligence. Megan looks forward to exploring how regular body scans can help her build a stronger connection between her mind and body, leading to greater clarity and resilience in her daily life.

Chapter 7: Mindful Movement and Activity

Mindful movement offers a doorway to harmony between body and mind. Combining physical exertion with mental awareness captivates those seeking an escape from life's tumultuous rhythm. Deliberate actions and presence can transform routine exercises into personal sanctuaries. This approach enhances physical health and nurtures a deeper connection to yourself, creating space for emotional tranquility amidst life's chaos.

In this chapter, readers will journey through ancient practices like yoga and Tai Chi that illuminate the path toward mindful movement. Explore how these movements are intricately tied to breathwork, creating a symphony of focus and relaxation that calms the mind. As you delve deeper, you'll discover how everyday activities such as walking or cycling become meditative experiences when approached with intention. The discussion extends to how these techniques foster community connections, enhance emotional resilience, and promote a balanced lifestyle. Whether you're drawn to group sessions or solo practice, this chapter offers insights into harnessing the power of mindful movement to cultivate a more prosperous, centered way of living.

How can mindful movement create a stronger connection between your body and mind, and how might this impact your overall well-being?

Incorporating Yoga and Tai Chi

In pursuing holistic well-being, yoga and Tai Chi are potent conduits for enhancing mindfulness through purposeful movement and breath. In these ancient arts, each movement is a physical exercise and an opportunity to engage deeply with the present moment.

Yoga, characterized by sequences of poses called 'asanas,' offers you a chance to delve into mindful sequencing. This approach allows each pose to be embraced as a meditative experience. As you transition from one asana to the next, you become immersed in a flow state, a harmonious rhythm where the mind quiets and becomes present. This flow encourages a harmonious relationship between body, mind, and spirit. Instead of rushing through movements, practitioners are encouraged to savor each transition, cultivating patience and self-awareness. For example, moving through sun salutations with deliberate slowness enables participants to notice subtle shifts in balance and alignment, fostering a deeper connection to one's bodily sensations and capabilities.

A significant aspect of yoga and Tai Chi is the synchronization of breath with movement. The breath acts as a rope to the now, anchoring practitioners firmly in their current experience. You can achieve deeper relaxation and peace through pranayama or controlled breathing techniques. Pranayama focuses on the length and depth of each breath, which can substantially calm the nervous system and reduce stress (Art, 2023). Practitioners forge a bridge between their inner selves and outer actions by consciously linking inhalations and exhalations with specific movements. This practice not only aids in maintaining concentration but also helps dissipate mental clutter, allowing for a serene, uninterrupted engagement with the present.

Tai Chi, a gentle martial art from ancient China, emphasizes slow and deliberate movements that weave balance and emotional steadiness into everyday life. These graceful, flowing motions are akin to meditation in motion, promoting the visualization of energy flow, or 'qi.' Practitioners of Tai Chi often describe an enhanced awareness of internal energy pathways, leading to improved physical and emotional harmony. Through Tai Chi, individuals learn to visualize their energy as a continuous, flowing stream, which grounds them physically and builds resilience against external stressors. Studies show that regular Tai Chi practice improves balance, flexibility, and cardiovascular health, improving stress management and mental clarity (Department of Health & Human Services, 2015).

One of the most transformative aspects of integrating mindful movement practices such as yoga and Tai Chi into daily routines is the tangible increase in calmness and stress management they promote. Regular practitioners report a heightened ability to cope with daily stressors, primarily attributed to intentional movement and breathwork grounding. Engaging in these practices provides a sanctuary for the mind, exposing it to periods of tranquility amidst the chaos of everyday life. Over time, this leads to a more balanced emotional state, where reactions to stress become measured and thoughtful rather than impulsive.

Furthermore, these practices cultivate an enhanced sense of emotional balance. As practitioners become more attuned to their bodies and minds through consistent training, they often experience increased self-acceptance. The journey of mindful movement is not about achieving perfection but embracing progress. This mindset shift extends beyond practice sessions, influencing interactions and decisions throughout life. With reduced anxiety and more excellent emotional stability, many find themselves better equipped to navigate challenges and maintain harmonious relationships.

The rhythmic quality inherent in yoga and Tai Chi movements further supports mindfulness by fostering concentration and focus. Each session becomes an opportunity to tune into one's thoughts and feelings without judgment. As individuals become more adept at concentrating during practice, this skill naturally translates into other areas of life, enhancing cognitive function and decision-making capabilities.

How could you incorporate the principles of yoga or Tai Chi into your daily routine to promote mindfulness and emotional balance?

Awareness During Walking or Exercise

Cultivating mindfulness during walking, running, or cycling transforms these activities into powerful tools for mental well-being. Walking meditation involves synchronizing your steps with your breath. This enhances sensory engagement and creates a serene space for reflection beyond structured thought. For example, imagine walking in a park and consciously placing each foot on the ground while inhaling and exhaling deeply. With every step, you become attuned to the sound of leaves rustling, the touch of a gentle breeze on your skin, and the rhythm of your heartbeat. This form of mindfulness allows you to be present, letting go of stress and distractions while embracing the moment fully.

Mindful running or cycling offers an escape from the constant stream of thoughts that often flood our minds. These activities naturally induce a rhythmic flow that encourages us to focus on our body's sensations. Whether it's feeling the impact of your feet against the ground or noticing the wind rushing past as you cycle, these experiences anchor you in the now. By focusing on the repetitive motion and physical sensations, you reduce overthinking and enter a meditative state. This practice isn't about achieving a specific pace or distance but finding rhythm and presence in movement.

Attuning to physical signals during exercise fosters a deeper connection with yourself and enhances health management. When you engage in mindful activity, you listen to what your body tells you. Are there areas of tension or ease? Do you feel energized or fatigued? Such awareness provides valuable insights into your physical condition and emotional state. By being conscious of these signals, you make informed decisions about how to best care for your body, whether by adjusting your routine, resting when needed, or pushing a little harder to challenge your limits. This self-awareness extends beyond exercise, nurturing a holistic understanding of your well-being.

Social mindfulness in group exercises further enriches this experience by creating community support, decreasing feelings of isolation, and deepening personal awareness. Participating in group runs or cycling sessions brings together individuals who share a common purpose. This collective energy fosters a sense of belonging and camaraderie, enhancing the enjoyment of the activity. Together, you share moments of achievement, encourage each other, and build meaningful connections that transcend the exercise. Engaging mindfully in group settings also sharpens your awareness of interpersonal dynamics, teaching empathy and understanding as you synchronize with others' paces and rhythms.

Research supports the idea that integrating mindfulness into regular physical activity promotes more consistent participation in moderate- to vigorous-intensity physical activity (MVPA). Mindfulness has been linked to better emotional regulation, reduced symptoms of depression and anxiety, and improved motivation for maintaining an active lifestyle (Payton Solk et al., 2023). For example, participating in a running club that emphasizes mindfulness can transform each session into a shared journey toward mental clarity and resilience, making it easier to adhere to MVPA guidelines despite busy schedules or fluctuating motivation levels.

Moreover, the benefits of mindful movement extend to those seeking personal growth and enhanced emotional intelligence. By practicing mindfulness during physical activities, individuals cultivate skills that help them cope with stressors in various life aspects. Emotional intelligence grows as one becomes more attuned to internal emotions and external environments, enhancing relationships and communication skills.

There are no strict rules for practicing mindfulness during exercise, which makes it accessible and adaptable to any lifestyle. You might set an intention before starting, focus on your breath throughout your workout, or periodically scan your body for sensations as you move. The key lies in paying attention with curiosity and openness, allowing each moment to unfold naturally. The ultimate goal is to integrate mindfulness into your exercise routine, transforming it into a nourishing ritual that empowers both body and mind.

How can turning everyday activities like walking or cycling into mindful experiences help you reduce stress and become more present in your daily life?

Leveraging Everyday Activities

Integrating mindfulness into daily activities transforms mundane tasks into increased presence and awareness opportunities. These practices remind us that mindfulness is about fully engaging in the present moment throughout our day.

Mindful Eating: Heightening Satisfaction

Eating mindfully can enhance our dining experience, promoting greater satisfaction and healthier eating choices. Often, meals are hurried, with little attention paid to flavors or textures. Slowing down and focusing on each bite can cultivate a deeper appreciation for your food. Begin by setting aside distractions such as phones or computers. As you eat, notice the colors and aromas of your meal. Chew slowly and allow your taste buds to savor the complex flavors and varied textures. This makes eating more enjoyable and helps you become more attuned to your body's hunger and fullness cues, leading to better portion control and healthier choices (Sandstrom, 2024).

Routine Chores as Meditative Practices

you often treat routine chores like doing dishes or folding laundry as tedious tasks to rush through. However, approaching these activities with mindfulness can turn them into meditative practices that engage all our senses. Consider the sound of running water while washing dishes or the fabric texture as you fold clothes. Focus on the rhythm and movement involved rather than the end goal. This shift in perspective allows you to find peace in repetitive actions, reducing stress and bringing a sense of calm and achievement to everyday life. Mindfulness during chores helps break the cycle of autopilot living, encouraging you to remain present and appreciative of each moment.

Commute Mindfulness: Breathing and Engagement

Commuting, whether by car or public transport, is often considered a necessary but stressful part of the day. Instead, view it as an opportunity for mindfulness practice. If you drive, notice the feel of the steering wheel, the sounds around you, and the pace of your breath. For those using public transportation, a simple breathing exercise can be profound. Try inhaling deeply for four counts, holding for four, and exhaling for four. This exercise reduces stress and improves focus, turning travel time into a personal retreat. Also, can you observe your surroundings, the changing scenery, or the interactions around you? Engaging in this way transforms commuting into a mindful journey, offering moments of peace amidst the hustle.

Mindfulness in Conversations: Enhancing Connections

Conversations can become superficial in today's fast-paced world, with distractions often taking precedence over genuine interaction. Mindful conversations emphasize active listening and minimizing distractions, fostering deeper connections and understanding. When someone speaks, listen intently without planning your response. Allow pauses and silence to occur naturally, making space for reflection. Being present with others strengthens relationships and enhances empathy and compassion as you truly hear and understand their perspectives. By committing to this practice, you're contributing to more meaningful and fulfilling interactions.

How could you apply mindfulness to routine tasks such as eating, doing chores, or commuting to enhance focus and find calm amidst daily activities?

Physical Movement as Emotional Release

Understanding emotional energy means recognizing how our bodies are barometers for the mind's unspoken tensions. Physical signs like tightened shoulders or a furrowed brow can signal stress or anxiety. Recognizing these signs is the first step to addressing emotional blocks. Movement naturally releases this tension, transforming silent signals into expressive gestures for a cathartic release.

Movement, particularly creative forms such as dance, holds transformative power. Dance serves as a channel for emotional expression that transcends verbal communication. Whether through improvisation or structured choreography, dance allows individuals to articulate feelings that might be nebulous or challenging to describe with words. Moving creatively to music fosters joy and connection, offering an enchanting blend of physical exertion and emotional liberation. This dual benefit not only enhances one's mood but also deepens the connection to oneself and others, creating a welcoming space for shared experiences and camaraderie (Dance as a Tool for Emotional Expression and Self-Management, n.d.).

Functional movement introduces another layer to emotional regulation. High-energy workouts such as aerobics, kickboxing, or circuit training channel stress into constructive action. In settings where these activities are practiced, individuals come together, fostering a sense of community support and collective strength. They empower participants, encouraging them to push physical boundaries while breaking down mental hurdles. This empowerment is not merely physical; it extends into everyday life, providing participants with the resilience to face personal challenges head-on. The communal aspect of such practices offers additional benefits, as mutual encouragement and shared goals enhance motivation and contribute to overall well-being.

Expressive exercises bridge intensity with emotional release, allowing one to explore emotions consciously. Practices like intense yoga flows or vigorous Pilates routines encourage participants to lose themselves in the movement. There is a synergy between breath and muscle, creating an internal dialogue that promotes introspection during exercise. By allowing participants to exert their total energy, these exercises help uncover insights and foster emotional clarity once the session has ended. Linking physical intensity to emotional release grants individuals a newfound understanding of their sensations and reactions, equipping them with tools to manage their emotions effectively.

To truly harness mindful movement's emotional and psychological benefits, a guideline emerges around listening to one's body. Individuals need to tune into their body's cues. Acknowledging fatigue, embracing bursts of energy, and being aware of discomfort or tension. This practice cultivates a heightened self-awareness that prevents injury and aligns physical movements with emotional needs, ensuring a balanced exercise and personal health approach. This alignment fosters a profound sense of presence, enhancing the effectiveness of movement-based mindfulness techniques.

The creative movement demands guidance on balancing structure with spontaneity. Participants should feel encouraged to explore their instincts within the broad framework of a routine, allowing room for personal innovation and adaptation. This balance nurtures creativity and ensures that the activity remains engaging and beneficial, avoiding monotony while promoting consistent engagement with the practice over time.

Clear guidelines on pacing and progression can benefit functional movement practices. Participants should gradually increase workout intensity to match their evolving capabilities, ensuring safety while maximizing benefits. Incorporating rest days and varied routines can prevent burnout and sustain motivation, making regular practice a sustainable part of lifestyle changes that support long-term emotional health and fitness.

Finally, in expressive exercise regimes, guiding participants to reflect on their emotional state before and after sessions can deepen insights gained from the experience. Journaling or meditating after exercise can crystallize discoveries, turning fleeting insights into lasting personal growth. This reflective process empowers individuals to carry the lessons learned during physical activity into broader areas, promoting continuous emotional development.

How can engaging in expressive physical activities, such as dance or functional movement, help you release pent-up emotions and improve mental clarity?

Summary and Reflections

This chapter delves into the transformative power of movement-based mindfulness techniques such as yoga and Tai Chi. These ancient practices are more than just physical exercises; they are gateways to deeper awareness, aligning breath with movement to foster a balanced mind-body connection. Through purposeful practices, individuals can engage in a journey of self-discovery and presence. We've explored how these activities, whether through structured sequences or fluid motions, offer an oasis of calm in the chaos of daily life. By combining mindful breathing with intentional movements, practitioners cultivate patience and emotional steadiness, enriching their mental well-being and enhancing resilience.

Furthermore, we've seen how everyday exercises like walking or cycling can become pathways to mindfulness when approached with intention and focus. Simple acts like synchronizing steps with breath transform routine physical activity into a meditative practice that enhances sensory engagement and promotes mental clarity. Engaging in group activities not only builds community but also enriches personal awareness through shared experiences. This chapter highlights mindful movement, which is not about reaching perfection but about embracing progression and fostering a greater sense of self-acceptance and emotional balance. Integrating these practices into your routine opens doors to improved emotional intelligence and stress management, allowing you to gracefully navigate life's challenges.

How do you envision integrating mindful movement practices into your life to foster emotional resilience and enrich your daily experiences?

Here's what Megan took away from the chapter:

Megan found this chapter on mindful movement incredibly insightful, as it presented new ways to connect her physical activities with her mental and emotional well-being. She was particularly intrigued by the idea that yoga and Tai Chi aren't just about stretching or physical health but about finding a more profound balance between mind and body. The emphasis on combining breathwork with movement resonated with her, as it reminded her that even her morning stretches could be more meaningful if done mindfully.

Megan loved the section on how even walking or cycling can become meditative experiences when she focuses on the sensations in her body and her breath. She could easily imagine herself turning her daily walks into mini-meditation sessions, where instead of worrying about her to-do list, she would focus on the feeling of each step, the rhythm of her breathing, and the sights and sounds around her. This felt like a simple yet powerful way to bring peace and presence into her day.

Using physical movement to release pent-up emotions was another eye-opener for Megan. She often feels stress build up in her body, especially her shoulders and neck, but she hadn't thought about how activities like dance or vigorous yoga could help her release those emotions. The suggestion to explore creative movements like dance felt liberating to her, as it seemed like a fun and expressive way to process feelings that are otherwise difficult to articulate.

The chapter also highlighted the importance of social mindfulness during group exercises, which Megan found interesting. She realized that joining a yoga or cycling group could help her stay active and build a sense of community. This social aspect of mindful movement felt like an exciting way to combine self-care with personal connections, which she values deeply.

Megan's biggest takeaway was realizing that she doesn't need to carve out extra time for mindfulness. It can be woven into her everyday activities. Whether she's commuting, doing household chores, or going for a walk, she now sees how to use these moments to be more present and calm, which could help reduce her stress and improve her mental clarity.

Moving forward, Megan plans to start small by incorporating mindful walking into her routine. She's also excited to explore yoga more deeply, focusing on her breath and being fully present during each pose. For Megan, this chapter opened up new possibilities for how she can take better care of her mental and emotional health through physical movement, and she's eager to see how it can help her feel more balanced and resilient in her everyday life.

Chapter 8: Building Sustainable Mindfulness Habits

Many undertake the endeavor of building sustainable mindfulness habits to weave mindfulness seamlessly into their lives. While mindfulness promises mental clarity and emotional peace, integrating it sustainably can feel daunting. Each day unfolds with its unique rhythm, and finding space for mindfulness within this flow requires intention and creativity. By nurturing these habits, you open the path to personal growth, fostering a deeper connection to yourself and the world around you.

In this chapter, readers will find guidance on creating a mindfulness practice that aligns with their lifestyle. The discussion will explore designing personalized schedules that transform mindful moments from sporadic occurrences into daily rituals. By understanding and respecting individual routines, readers will learn how to identify opportune times for short, impactful mindfulness exercises. Flexibility will be emphasized as a cornerstone for maintaining these practices amidst life's unpredictable demands, ensuring they remain a source of relief rather than stress. Furthermore, practical tools like digital reminders and journaling will be explored for their role in supporting consistency and reflection. This chapter aims to offer a comprehensive exploration of tools and strategies that make mindfulness an enriching part of everyday life, ultimately enhancing overall mental health and emotional well-being.

What small mindfulness practices can you integrate into your daily routine to make them more consistent and sustainable?

Amelie Brooks

Creating a Personal Schedule

Designing a personalized mindfulness schedule can transform integrating mindful practices into daily life into something manageable and sustainable. Understanding your unique lifestyle and demands allows you to seamlessly introduce mindfulness moments that enhance mental health and emotional well-being.

The first step is to analyze your daily routines to identify potential time slots for mindfulness activities. These moments don't need to be lengthy; short increments, like 5-10 minutes in the morning or before bed, can have profound effects when practiced consistently. Short increments, like 5-10 minutes in the morning or before bed, can have profound effects when practiced consistently. To assist with this process, try keeping a journal for a week to log your activities. Note instances where you are waiting. In line at the store, during your commute, or even while brewing your morning coffee. These seemingly insignificant moments are perfect opportunities to integrate mindfulness practices. Thoughtful scheduling ensures regular practice and prevents mindfulness from becoming an additional stressor (Hong, 2023).

Flexibility is crucial to sustaining these practices amid the unpredictability of daily life. Instead of rigidly adhering to fixed times, allow for fluidity in your schedule. Adjust your mindfulness sessions accordingly if a meeting runs late or other responsibilities arise. The goal is to incorporate mindfulness without it feeling like another obligation. Understanding that some days will be more demanding than others encourages adaptability and reduces frustration. This approach promotes a sense of balance and respect for both personal and professional demands.

It's essential to set realistic mindfulness goals. While aspirations of meditating for an hour every day are admirable, they might only be feasible for some initially. Begin with small, attainable goals, such as practicing mindfulness for five minutes daily. As you become comfortable and notice the benefits, gradually increase your practice duration and diversify your techniques. Setting achievable goals helps avoid burnout and keeps motivation high. Celebrating small victories, like completing a week of consistent practice, can reinforce positive habits and lift spirits.

To maintain a consistent schedule, consider using digital tools and journaling. Apps for meditation and mindfulness can remind you of your practice times and offer guided sessions tailored to varying durations. They often provide tracking features and statistics about your progress, which can motivate continued engagement. Journaling, whether digitally or on paper, is another valuable tool. Writing about your experiences reinforces the habit and invites reflection on what works best for you and how mindfulness impacts your well-being over time. Engaging in this reflective practice supports deeper personal insights and emotional growth (Rosebud - AI Journal for Personal Growth, n.d.).

Incorporating these strategies into daily life creates a framework that supports mindfulness integration without overwhelming the practitioner. Remember, the journey of mindfulness is intensely personal; what works for one person may not work for another. Therefore, allowing room for personalization within these guidelines ensures that each individual's unique needs and circumstances are addressed.

How can you design a flexible mindfulness schedule that fits seamlessly into your lifestyle without adding extra stress?

Overcoming Obstacles Like Time

In today's fast-paced world, dedicating time to mindfulness can seem a formidable challenge. However, making room for this practice is crucial in enhancing mental well-being and emotional resilience. You can begin by identifying non-essential activities that consume large chunks of your day. This might include excessive screen time, prolonged social media scrolling, or non-urgent commitments. By recognizing these habits, you can allocate some of this time toward mindfulness practices, offering more substantial benefits to your mental health.

To seamlessly incorporate mindfulness into daily routines, consider the concept of micro-mindfulness. Brief moments of awareness that can be embedded during transitions or breaks throughout the day. For instance, taking a minute to focus on breathing while waiting in line, savoring the taste and texture of a meal instead of eating hastily, or stepping outside for a moment's quiet reflection between meetings can foster a sense of calm and presence. These small, intentional acts cultivate mindfulness without requiring additional time, making them attractive to those with hectic schedules.

A key strategy for overcoming time constraints is setting flexible expectations. Rather than aiming for long meditation sessions, begin with short, quality-focused practices that prioritize clarity and attentiveness over duration. Understanding that any amount of mindfulness is beneficial can alleviate the pressure to meet rigid self-imposed standards. It's about the journey, not perfection. This approach encourages individuals to appreciate the quality of their mindfulness experiences, thus fostering a positive mindset towards regular practice.

Engaging with a community is invaluable in maintaining your commitment to mindfulness. Engaging with others through group sessions, online forums, or local workshops provides opportunities to share experiences, learn from peers, and absorb different perspectives. The camaraderie and encouragement in these spaces can significantly boost motivation, especially when obstacles arise. Community interactions create a shared learning environment where participants feel supported and inspired to continue their mindfulness journey.

What non-essential activities in your daily routine could you reduce to make more time for mindfulness, and how might this improve your overall well-being?

Maintaining Motivation and Consistency

Sustaining enthusiasm for regular mindfulness practice can be challenging, but by embedding personal meaning into it, your practice becomes a meaningful ritual that resonates deeply with you. To start, ask yourself: Why were you drawn to mindfulness initially? Was it to manage stress, find peace, or enhance self-awareness? By aligning your practice with these personal motivators, mindfulness gains intrinsic value, making it easier to stay committed. For example, if your goal is to reduce anxiety, remind yourself how each session contributes to that purpose. This reflection can inspire a more profound engagement as you witness tangible improvements in your mental and emotional state.

Celebrating milestones, no matter how small, is another essential strategy to sustain enthusiasm. Just as in any journey, you'll need to acknowledge your progress. These celebrations do not have to be grand; they could be as simple as treating yourself to a favorite activity or reflecting on how far you've come since you began. Setting small, achievable goals along the way allows for frequent celebrations. Perhaps aim to practice daily mindfulness for one week or try a specific meditation technique for a month. As you achieve these objectives, take time to recognize your growth, which can reinforce your motivation and provide a tangible record of your journey.

Variety is crucial when maintaining long-term engagement with mindfulness practices. Many practitioners need help with challenges such as boredom or fatigue if their routines become too predictable. By introducing different mindfulness techniques, you keep the practice fresh and engaging. Explore varied forms like guided meditations, mindfulness walks, or breathing exercises. Each method offers unique benefits and keeps your practice dynamic. For instance, if seated meditation feels monotonous, try walking or mindful yoga to revitalize your sessions. Diversifying your approach can prevent practice fatigue and reengage the interest that initially drew you to mindfulness.

Reflecting regularly on the benefits gained from mindfulness is vital for maintaining motivation. Consider setting aside weekly moments to journal about noticeable changes in your mindset, energy levels, or emotional responses. Over time, this reflection will reveal improvement patterns and remind you of mindfulness's positive impact on your life. You may find that you sleep better, feel less stressed, or handle conflicts more calmly. Such reflections serve as evidence of progress and can fuel your desire to continue with the practice.

While using various strategies to sustain enthusiasm is essential, remember that mindfulness is flexible. There's no rigid way to practice. It's about finding what works best for you and adapting as necessary. Personalization allows mindfulness to become a sustainable habit rather than a burdensome task. Engage with your practice creatively, and don't hesitate to modify techniques to suit your evolving needs or interests.

Finally, sharing your experiences with others can also bolster your motivation. Joining mindfulness communities or discussion groups provides opportunities to learn new approaches and exchange insights. Hearing about others' journeys can be inspiring and offer fresh perspectives on navigating challenges. This communal support can make your practice feel like a shared endeavor rather than a solitary pursuit, enhancing accountability and enjoyment.

How can aligning your mindfulness practice with your personal goals and motivations help you stay consistent and engaged over time?

Amelie Brooks

Evaluating Growth and Adjustments

Evaluating and adjusting mindfulness practices is crucial for sustainable personal growth. At its core, mindfulness is about being present and fully engaging with the moment. Yet, as with any personal development practice, continuous evaluation and adjustments are essential to ensure these practices remain practical and relevant.

Implementing systems tracking your progress and emotional responses can be a compass in your mindfulness journey. Many individuals find it helpful to maintain a journal where they record their daily mindfulness activities, noting how they feel before and after each session. This tracking allows you to observe patterns over time, identify stress or anxiety triggers, and understand which mindfulness techniques bring you the most peace or clarity. For example, someone might notice that a short morning meditation sets a positive tone for their day or that practicing mindful breathing helps calm their nerves before a challenging meeting. Documenting these observations provides tangible reflections and reinforces progress, motivating further commitment.

In addition to tracking, reassessing and adapting techniques ensures ongoing relevance and effectiveness. Mindfulness isn't one-size-fits-all; what works at one stage might not be effective later. Regularly revisiting and evaluating one's mindfulness practices can breathe new life into routines that have become stale or ineffective. Integrating new forms of mindfulness, such as mindful walking or body scans, might offer fresh perspectives and boost engagement. Alternatively, adjusting the duration or timing of practices could better align with changing schedules or energy levels, ensuring they seamlessly fit into daily life.

Seeking feedback from mentors or groups adds another valuable layer to personal mindfulness practice. Engaging with experienced practitioners offers insights that might not be apparent when practicing in isolation. Mentors can provide guidance on overcoming common hurdles or suggest adjustments based on their experiences. Furthermore, group settings create an environment of shared learning, where exchanging stories or challenges fosters community and support. These interactions often lead to newfound motivation and innovative ideas, helping individuals recognize blind spots in their practice and encouraging more purposeful engagement.

After facing disruptions, reinforcing dedication by reconnecting with initial motivations is vital. Life's unpredictability can temporarily sideline one's mindfulness journey, especially during stress or significant life changes. During these periods, reflecting on why one began practicing mindfulness can reignite the passion and purpose behind the habit. Revisiting initial motivations - perhaps written down or visualized - can be a powerful reminder of the benefits mindfulness brought or promised to bring, such as reduced stress, improved focus, or enhanced emotional resilience. This reflection reestablishes connection and strengthens resolve to resume and sustain practices despite life's challenges.

How can regular reflection and evaluation of your mindfulness journey help you identify what's working well and what might need adjustment to keep your practice fresh and compelling?

Amelie Brooks

Summary and Reflections

Embracing mindfulness in daily life might initially seem daunting, but it's a journey worth taking. This chapter delves into creating a personal mindfulness schedule that seamlessly fits into everyday routines, aiming to enhance mental health and emotional well-being. These practices gradually become second nature by carving out small moments for mindfulness, whether during a morning coffee brew or a brief pause while waiting in line. The key lies in flexibility; rather than rigidly adhering to specific times, allow adjustments based on the day's demands. This approach makes mindfulness manageable and turns it into a nurturing habit instead of an added stressor.

As you navigate life's hustle, it's easy to feel overwhelmed by the pressure to do more. Yet, this chapter reminds us that sustainable mindfulness isn't about perfection or lengthy meditation sessions. It's about finding balance, setting realistic goals, and celebrating small victories. Utilizing tools like digital reminders or journaling can offer support and encourage reflection, helping you understand what methods work best for you. Each mindful moment builds upon the last, contributing to resilience and fostering personal growth. By embracing these practices uniquely suited to your needs, mindfulness becomes a meaningful part of your life, offering peace and clarity amidst the chaos.

What strategies from this chapter can you implement to transform mindfulness into a sustainable habit that enriches your life daily?

Here's what Megan learned from reading the chapter:

Megan found this chapter about building sustainable mindfulness habits particularly helpful, as it addressed her biggest challenge: consistency. She has always wanted to incorporate mindfulness into her life more regularly but has struggled to stick with it amid her busy schedule. What resonated most with her was the idea of flexibility. She realized that her previous attempts at mindfulness felt rigid, which often discouraged her when she couldn't meet her self-imposed expectations.

She appreciated the suggestion of starting small, like integrating 5-10 minutes of mindfulness during moments that would otherwise be spent scrolling on her phone or mindlessly going through her day. She was especially drawn to the concept of "micro-mindfulness," as it seems practical to cultivate awareness without needing long, uninterrupted sessions. Megan could imagine using these micro-mindful moments while waiting for her coffee to brew or during her commute to center herself and reconnect with the present moment.

The chapter also introduced Megan to the importance of celebrating small wins. It had never occurred to her to pause and recognize her progress, even if it was just practicing mindfulness for five days. This shift in mindset made her feel more empowered to approach her practice without feeling overwhelmed by perfectionism.

Another insight that stood out to Megan was personalizing her mindfulness journey. The chapter encouraged her to try different forms of mindfulness, like body scans or mindful walking, to keep things fresh and prevent boredom. She feels inspired to explore new techniques and experiment with what fits best into her routine rather than sticking to the same daily practice.

Megan also resonated with the idea of journaling about her mindfulness journey. Writing down her feelings after each session could help her track patterns, notice the benefits, and reflect on what's working. She liked the idea that journaling could remind her of her progress, especially on days when mindfulness feels more like a chore than a relief.

Moving forward, Megan plans to start practicing micro-mindfulness throughout her day, setting the goal to practice for just 5 minutes each morning. She's also excited to use an app to help remind her to pause for mindful moments. For Megan, this chapter was a turning point, showing her that mindfulness doesn't have to be perfect or rigid. It can be adaptable, manageable, and deeply personal.

Chapter 9: Real-Life Applications and Benefits

Mindfulness is more than a concept; it's a way of life that offers tangible benefits in real-world situations. Practicing mindfulness can profoundly change how you interact with others and handle daily stressors, whether at work, home, or personal relationships. By approaching each moment with full attention and presence, mindfulness helps unravel modern life's complexities, making space for joy, clarity, and calm. In a time where distractions abound, it serves as a gentle reminder to pause, breathe, and focus on what truly matters.

In this chapter, you explore the transformative power of mindfulness across diverse aspects of life. We'll delve into its practical applications in the workplace and relationships, illustrating how mindful practices like meditative pauses and active listening can foster a more harmonious environment. The chapter will also shed light on strategies to integrate mindfulness into daily routines, from breathing exercises to mindful walking, offering readers easy-to-implement tools for managing stress and enhancing well-being. Packed with relatable success stories and insights, this exploration will underscore the myriad benefits of mindfulness, inspiring readers to embark on their journey towards mental clarity and emotional resilience.

How can I begin incorporating mindfulness into my daily life to experience greater clarity and calm?

Amelie Brooks

Applying Mindfulness at Work

The pressure to perform and succeed can be overwhelming in today's fast-paced work environment. Integrating mindfulness into daily work enhances focus, productivity, and overall well-being. This approach isn't just about individual benefit; it can transform team dynamics and foster a healthier workplace culture.

Mindful meetings are a perfect starting point for incorporating mindfulness at work. Communication can become more effective by introducing mindfulness techniques like brief meditative pauses or setting clear intentions at the beginning of a meeting. Participants are more present, listen attentively, and engage with one another constructively, reducing misunderstandings and fostering collaboration. These mindful approaches create an atmosphere where ideas flow freely and everyone feels valued and heard.

Moreover, the workplace can be a breeding ground for stress, which often undermines our ability to concentrate and be productive. Simple practices, like mindful breathing exercises during breaks, offer practical solutions. Taking a few deep breaths encourages us to center ourselves, easing tension and stress accumulated throughout the day. This practice helps employees reset their focus, improving concentration and clarity in tackling tasks. It's a powerful tool that empowers individuals to handle challenges calmly and efficiently.

Leadership plays a crucial role in cultivating mindfulness in the organization. When leaders model mindfulness, they demonstrate emotional intelligence and resilience, which are essential for inspiring their teams. Mindful leaders are attuned to their own emotions and those of others, fostering an environment where empathy and understanding thrive. This creates a space where team members feel supported and motivated to contribute their best, ultimately leading to better team dynamics and collaborative success.

Beyond improving focus and reducing stress, mindfulness has the potential to unlock creativity. Being mindful in a world filled with constant distractions clears the mental clutter and allows creative thoughts to surface. It enables individuals to tap into their imaginations without the noise of self-doubt or external pressures. Whether through short meditation sessions or simply dedicating time to reflect, mindfulness helps open the mind to new ideas and innovative solutions. This enhanced creativity can be a significant advantage in fields that rely on fresh and inventive approaches.

Several guidelines exist for readers interested in bringing mindfulness into their workplaces. First, identify the specific needs of your workplace and tailor mindfulness practices accordingly. Start small by integrating short meditation periods or breathing exercises into daily routines, especially during meetings and breaks. Encourage leaders to lead by example, embracing mindfulness in their leadership style to inspire others. Create opportunities for employees to share their experiences and insights, further building a mindfulness community within the organization.

What small mindfulness practices can I introduce into my workday to reduce stress and increase focus?

Amelie Brooks

Improving Relationships Through Presence

In the hustle and bustle of our daily lives, you often overlook the simple yet profound impact that mindfulness can have on our relationships. Practicing active listening is a foundational way mindfulness enriches your interactions with others. Engaging in mindful communication creates a space where others feel heard and valued, fostering trust and understanding.

Imagine sitting across from a friend or colleague, your full attention directed towards them. This isn't just about hearing words; it's about genuinely listening, picking up on their tone and body language nuances. By doing so, you validate their experiences and show empathy and respect. Mindful, active listening requires us to put aside distractions and judgments, allowing us to connect more deeply with those around us.

This practice is crucial today when technology often divides our attention. Picture a scenario where you're conversing with a friend but simultaneously scrolling through your phones. In such situations, the connection remains superficial. However, you open the door for authentic exchanges and understanding by being present, putting the devices away, and focusing entirely on the person in front of you. This level of engagement can transform relationships, making them more rewarding and fulfilling.

Mindfulness also enhances emotional connections through empathy. It encourages us to be fully present with ourselves and others, leading to stronger ties and conflict resolution. When individuals practice mindfulness, they become more attuned to their emotions and those of others, allowing them to communicate more peacefully. Think of a time when a discussion started escalating into an argument. A mindful approach might involve pausing, taking a deep breath, and refocusing on understanding rather than reacting. By employing empathy, conflicts can be defused, creating opportunities for constructive dialogue instead of discord.

Moreover, mindfulness helps us approach conflicts with a collaborative mindset. It's easy to become defensive in disagreements, often jeopardizing the relationship's integrity. But by staying present and open-minded, mindfulness facilitates a shift from adversarial stances to cooperative problem-solving. This doesn't mean disregarding your needs but aligning them with mutual goals. For instance, in workplace scenarios, approaching projects mindfully can lead to better team dynamics and shared success, as each member feels valued and respected.

Engaging fully with others in joint activities can also greatly enhance our connections. Often, you carry out tasks or spend time with people while mentally ticking off other things on your agenda. Mindfulness asks us to slow down and immerse ourselves in what's happening. Whether sharing a meal, collaborating on a work project, or simply being together, these moments become more poignant and enjoyable when fully present. They offer chances to appreciate shared experiences, laughter, and even silence, all contributing to the richness of interpersonal bonds.

Consider family gatherings where everyone seems glued to their screens, exchanging minimal conversation. Now, contrast this with a mindful gathering where phones are set aside, and every participant immerses themselves in discussions, games, or stories. The difference in the atmosphere is palpable. The latter setting fosters warmth, understanding, and lasting memories, reminding us why these interactions are precious.

Incorporating mindfulness into our relationships requires deliberate effort, yet the rewards are immense. By practicing active listening, enhancing empathy, embracing collaboration during conflicts, and cherishing shared experiences, you significantly elevate the quality of our connections. These practices do not demand drastic changes to how you live but rather subtle shifts in attention and intention.

Different tools and techniques can support this journey toward mindful communication. Practices like meditation, breathing exercises, and reflection can help center us, preparing us to engage more meaningfully with others. Regular meditation sharpens our ability to focus and listen attentively. Breathing exercises allow us to stay grounded, particularly during tense situations. Reflecting on conversations lets us evaluate what went well and where improvements may be needed, continually refining our relational skills.

Coupled with these practices, consistent reminders to remain present in conversations can lead to impactful results. Intentional pauses before responding, maintaining eye contact, and eliminating distractions, such as phones, cultivate an environment conducive to genuine connection. Through these efforts, relationships transition from transactional encounters to transformative experiences enriched with understanding and appreciation.

The benefits of adopting mindfulness extend beyond personal relationships to professional environments. Colleagues who practice mindful communication build harmonious workplaces, reducing misunderstandings and enhancing productivity. Such environments encourage innovation and collaboration, where every team member feels empowered to contribute and communicate freely.

Furthermore, embracing mindfulness in professional settings can be a model for others, inspiring workplace cultures that prize authenticity and respect. Leaders who consistently demonstrate empathy and presence establish rapport with their teams, fostering a supportive atmosphere that promotes well-being and satisfaction.

How can I be more present in my relationships to create deeper, more meaningful connections with those around me?

Dealing with Daily Stressors Effectively

Mindfulness is more than a trend; it's a practical tool that enhances your ability to manage daily stressors and life's challenges. For adults and young adults who often find themselves overwhelmed by anxiety, incorporating mindfulness into daily life can be transformative. Individuals can effectively mitigate overwhelming feelings and recharge their mental energy by intentionally pausing through short mindfulness practices. These mindful breaks require little time and can be easily implemented into the busiest schedules.

Set aside a few minutes daily to practice deep breathing or guided meditation. Such practices create an intentional pause, allowing for a moment of calm amid the rush of daily activities. These brief periods of mindfulness act as reset buttons for the mind, offering clarity and perspective. This simple yet powerful technique enables you to step back, assess your emotions, and respond rather than react to stressors.

Another significant aspect of mindfulness is its integration into everyday routines. Mundane activities, typically performed on autopilot, offer hidden opportunities for cultivating present-focused awareness and balance. Take, for example, mindful eating. This practice involves paying close attention to the sensory experiences of eating. Savoring each bite's flavors, textures, and aromas rather than rushing through meals distracted by screens or thoughts. Mindful eating fosters appreciation for food and promotes a healthier relationship with eating.

Similarly, incorporating mindfulness into walking transforms a routine task into an opportunity for grounding oneself in the present moment. Mindful walking focuses attention on each step, the contact of feet with the ground, and the rhythm of movement. Doing so becomes a practice that balances body and mind, providing a refreshing break from constant busyness while encouraging presence and attunement with one's surroundings.

Equipped with mindfulness tools, individuals become better prepared to handle stress. Recognizing and acknowledging your responses to situations, rather than letting them pass unnoticed, is integral to building resilience against stressors. When faced with a challenging situation, applying mindfulness allows for observing internal reactions. It emphasizes acknowledging emotions without judgment, creating space for thoughtful decision-making.

This conscious engagement with emotional responses strengthens mental resilience, making it easier to adapt to changing circumstances. Individuals can navigate challenges calmly and clearly rather than being swept away by stress and anxiety. Enhanced resilience doesn't mean eliminating stress but developing an improved capacity to cope with its effects, ultimately fostering more excellent emotional stability.

Practicing mindfulness regularly contributes profoundly to this process of resilience building. Over time, consistent mindfulness practice fortifies mental resilience, supporting adaptability and emotional stability. Engaging in mindfulness exercises daily, whether through meditation, mindful walks, or even mindful breathing, ingrains these habits into one's lifestyle, creating an ever-present resource for managing stress.

Despite varying personal circumstances, the benefits of mindfulness remain accessible. Transitioning from awareness to action represents a crucial step in utilizing mindfulness effectively. As research supports, meditation programs provide small to moderate reductions in psychological stress, suggesting its viability in stress management (Goyal et al., 2014). Professionals endorse mindfulness-based interventions due to their positive impact on both emotional and physical symptoms associated with stress, anxiety, and depression.

For those embarking on their mindfulness journey, guidelines can help structure initial efforts. Starting with brief sessions, such as five minutes daily, eases integration into routines without becoming burdensome. Gradually increasing the duration encourages deeper immersion into the practice. Additionally, using apps or online resources designed for beginners can offer guidance and support, making mindfulness exploration more approachable and less daunting.

Ultimately, mindfulness practices serve as invaluable allies in pursuing enhanced emotional intelligence and personal growth. By anchoring attention in the present, recognizing emotional responses, and cultivating balance, individuals transform everyday challenges into opportunities for growth. As mindfulness takes root, it nurtures a resilient mindset capable of weathering life's storms with grace and composure.

How can I use mindfulness to manage the daily stressors in my life better?

Success Stories and Case Studies

Imagine starting a journey filled with anxiety and self-doubt yet hoping for a change that leads to personal growth. This is where many people find themselves before embarking on their mindfulness journey. Personal stories from individuals across different walks of life offer a powerful testament to the transformative effects of mindfulness. These journeys highlight how mindfulness helped them combat overthinking and anxiety, showcasing its applications through various life phases.

Consider John, a middle-aged executive engulfed by stress and sleepless nights due to work pressures. He turned to mindfulness as a last resort, learning to focus his attention and intentions through meditation sessions. Over time, John noticed his mind slowly quieting during moments that once would have triggered panic. He became less reactive, which helped him at work and improved his relationships at home. His story underscores the universal struggle with mental stress and the profound impact mindfulness can have.

In younger demographics, like students, mindfulness offers a similar refuge. Megan, a college student, dealt with severe anxiety that affected her academic performance and social life. By integrating simple mindfulness practices into her daily routine, such as five-minute breathing exercises between classes, she managed to alleviate her symptoms. Her academic performance improved, and she gained the confidence to engage more deeply with her peers. Megan's journey shows how mindfulness can fit different life stages while addressing everyday challenges.

Mindfulness doesn't just benefit individuals; it can reshape entire organizational landscapes. In many businesses, cultivating a mindfulness culture has resulted in noteworthy transformations. For instance, consider a company with low employee morale and productivity dwindling. Introducing mindfulness workshops led to a remarkable shift. Employees who participated reported feeling more engaged and less stressed. The overall atmosphere became more positive, fostering collaboration and innovation, indicating how mindfulness can redefine business environments.

BlueBay Asset Management provides a concrete example. They implemented mindfulness programs aimed at enhancing decision-making and emotional intelligence. The results were impressive; employees enhanced their work output and developed better interpersonal skills, contributing to a collaborative workspace (Carter et al., 2016). Such case studies illustrate the potential for increased organizational productivity and resilience when mindfulness becomes part of the corporate ethos.

Mindfulness extends beyond personal and professional realms, reaching into communities as well. Schools and community centers have increasingly adopted mindfulness programs to improve collective well-being. These initiatives often lead to significant enhancements in mental health outcomes. In one school district, the introduction of mindfulness practices resulted in reduced student anxiety levels and improved concentration, which translated into better academic achievement. Teachers also noted a calmer, more focused learning environment. This positive shift demonstrates how mindfulness can be a potent tool for nurturing a healthier, more peaceful community.

Success narratives often span longer timeframes, revealing the sustained benefits of mindfulness practice. Take Sarah, a retiree who started her mindfulness practice later in life. Initially, she sought to cope with loneliness and depression after losing her partner. Through dedicated effort, Sarah's mindfulness journey transformed her sense of isolation into one of connection, with herself and others. Over the years, Sarah became a mentor within her community, advocating for mindfulness as a path to personal freedom and contentment. Her story highlights the long-term benefits and perpetual evolution that accompany ongoing mindfulness practice.

Such inspiring examples remind us that mindfulness is not merely a set of techniques; it's a way of being that fosters continual growth. As these personal journeys, organizational successes, and community programs reveal, the practice holds immense potential for transforming diverse aspects of life. Whether an individual seeks relief from anxiety or a corporation aims to foster a thriving workplace, the real-world benefits of mindfulness are both vast and profound. These narratives encourage exploring and adopting mindfulness practices, inspiring hope for sustainable personal evolution and collective well-being.

As you delve deeper into understanding mindfulness, it becomes evident that its transformative power stems from its adaptable nature and broad applicability. The stories shared in this section showcase the varied facets of mindfulness, reinforcing the notion that it can serve as a beacon during tumultuous times. Each journey is a compelling illustration of how mindfulness practices can catalyze monumental changes, no matter how modest they may begin. By reflecting on these examples, readers are encouraged to contemplate how integrating mindfulness into their lives might yield similarly rewarding experiences.

What aspects of these mindfulness success stories resonate with my challenges, and how can I apply similar practices?

Wrapping Up

Mindfulness, as explored in this chapter, offers a remarkable pathway to improving various facets of life through its practical application. Integrating mindfulness into the workplace and personal interactions allows individuals to transform stress-filled environments into havens of focus and collaboration. Through simple practices like mindful breathing or active listening, you can cultivate a sense of presence that enhances productivity and strengthens relationships. These mindful moments are not just about individual betterment but have the potential to uplift entire teams and foster empathy and understanding in our connections with others.

As you engage with these concepts, it's evident that mindfulness is an approachable and effective tool for managing modern life's challenges. Whether dealing with workplace pressures or seeking deeper emotional connections, mindfulness techniques offer reliable support. The real-world benefits, from enhanced creativity to reduced stress and improved interpersonal dynamics, illustrate the transformative power of being present. By embracing these practices, even small steps can lead to profound changes, enabling you to live a more balanced and meaningful life.

What first step can I take today to integrate mindfulness into my personal and professional life?

Here's what Megan learned from reading the chapter:

Megan found this chapter particularly eye-opening, as it showcased the wide-ranging applications of mindfulness beyond individual practices. She was especially drawn to incorporating mindfulness into her daily interactions at work and with her friends and family. The example of mindful meetings resonated deeply with her, as she often felt that conversations at work were rushed and unfocused. She realized how beneficial it would be to introduce moments of mindfulness, such as setting intentions before meetings or taking short pauses to regroup. These small changes could foster better communication and reduce the anxiety she often feels during discussions.

The section on improving relationships through active listening also hit home for Megan. She recognized that she sometimes struggles to focus entirely during conversations, often distracted by her phone or thoughts. She appreciated the reminder that being present with others can lead to deeper, more meaningful connections. Putting away distractions and engaging fully with the person in front of her felt like a simple but powerful way to improve her relationships.

What stood out most was the concept of mindful walking and mindful eating. Megan often rushes through meals and walks without thinking, missing opportunities to relax and reset during her busy day. She realized she could find more balance and peace in her daily life by slowing down and paying attention to these routine activities. She also liked using these moments to reflect on her emotions and manage stress more effectively.

Megan found the success stories at the end of the chapter particularly inspiring. Hearing about people like John, who transformed his work life with mindfulness, and Sarah, who found peace and connection later in life, gave her hope that mindfulness could have a lasting impact on her challenges. These stories encouraged her to think about how to start small and gradually integrate mindfulness into her life to manage stress better and improve her relationships.

Moving forward, Megan plans to begin with mindful breathing exercises during her work breaks and to practice active listening during conversations. She also intends to be more present during meals and while walking, using these activities as opportunities to ground herself. This chapter made her feel more confident in her ability to incorporate mindfulness into her personal and professional life in manageable and meaningful ways.

Chapter 10: The Path to Inner Peace

Finding inner peace is a journey that involves embracing change through mindfulness. This pursuit isn't just about reaching a destination; it's about the transformations that occur along the way. Many face challenges like anxiety and overwhelm, which can cloud clarity and disrupt peace. Understanding oneself better through reflection and deliberate practice is the key to overcoming these hurdles. The concept of inner peace might seem elusive, but anyone can begin this transformative journey by taking steps to manage thoughts and emotions. Like nurturing a garden, with patience and care, the seeds of mindfulness grow into a serene and vibrant state of mind.

This chapter invites readers to explore various techniques designed to foster long-lasting peace and mental clarity. It begins with assessing personal transformations, understanding how previous experiences have shaped one's current state and leveraging this insight for growth. Mindfulness goals offer a pathway forward, guiding this journey towards tranquility. However, life inevitably presents setbacks, and learning strategies to handle these moments effectively ensures progress isn't derailed. Lastly, the importance of committing to lifelong mindfulness is emphasized, highlighting the ongoing nature of this endeavor. Through mindful journaling, setting realistic goals, navigating obstacles, and fostering a commitment to continuous practice, this chapter provides valuable tools for achieving a state of enduring calm.

What small changes can I make today to cultivate a more profound sense of inner peace and mental clarity?

Amelie Brooks

Assessing Personal Transformations

Reflecting on your personal growth through mindfulness can be profoundly transformative. At the heart of this journey is reflective journaling, a simple yet potent tool that serves as a mirror and a map, guiding us toward greater self-awareness and helping us track our evolution. Reflective journaling involves taking time each day or week to jot down thoughts, experiences, and feelings. By journaling, you record your journey, capturing moments of clarity, doubt, joy, and struggle.

Journaling enhances self-awareness by encouraging introspection about how you respond to life's challenges and triumphs. You might start by writing down three things that went well each day, and over time, patterns will emerge. For example, you may discover that you feel most fulfilled when spending time outdoors or challenged when tackling new tasks at work. This leads to deeper insights into your behaviors and emotions, helping you understand what truly matters and how to nurture those aspects for greater peace.

In addition to journaling, identifying milestones in your mindfulness practice is essential to celebrating significant achievements. Milestones act as progress markers, highlighting points where you've overcome challenges or introduced new mindfulness techniques into your routine. These could range from meditating consistently for a month to successfully applying mindfulness strategies in stressful situations. Each milestone reminds you of your journey's success and encourages continued commitment to personal growth.

As you continue to grow through mindfulness, gathering feedback from others offers invaluable external perspectives.

Although personal reflection is crucial, our self-assessment sometimes overlooks subtle changes that others can observe better. Whether through conversations with friends, family, or mentors, feedback can illuminate unseen shifts and validate your efforts. It also provides an opportunity to gain insights from others who have noticed positive changes in your demeanor or attitude. While you don't need to look for feedback constantly, I can tell you that you're reaching out can help you understand your progress.

Evaluating emotional states is another vital component of understanding personal growth through mindfulness. Mindfulness practice often leads to more effective emotional regulation, allowing individuals to recognize and handle their emotions constructively. Begin by paying attention to your emotional responses throughout the day, noting them in your journal. Consider questions such as: What feelings did I experience today? How did I react to them? Was there a specific trigger? Over time, you'll notice trends in your emotional landscape and can evaluate how mindfulness has helped shift these states. Acknowledging these shifts is critical to appreciating how far you've come and reinforcing the benefits of consistent mindfulness practice.

With each journal entry, milestone celebration, piece of feedback, and evaluation of your emotional state, the path to inner peace becomes clearer. These tools offer a method for tracking progress and serve as a compass for navigating future transformations. Achieving long-term mental clarity requires recognizing and embracing change; mindful reflection ensures these transformations are possible and celebrated.

Amelie Brooks

To illustrate the power of reflective journaling, consider the story of Emma, a young adult who frequently felt overwhelmed by anxiety and stress. Initially skeptical of journaling, Emma decided to try a simple practice of writing down her thoughts and feelings before bed. Within a few weeks, she began recognizing moments in her day where she reacted with undue stress, pinpointing specific triggers that led to these reactions. This newfound awareness allowed Emma to develop targeted mindfulness strategies, such as deep breathing exercises, to employ during stressful situations. Journaling became a safe space for Emma to explore her thoughts without judgment, ultimately empowering her to understand and manage her emotions more effectively.

For those embarking on a similar journey, it's helpful to establish guidelines for consistent journaling practices. Aim to set aside dedicated time each day or week, free from distractions, to write honestly about your experiences and emotions. Regularity is vital to gaining the full benefits of reflective journaling. Additionally, don't be afraid to experiment with different prompts or styles - whether focusing on gratitude, future aspirations, or emotional responses - to find what resonates best with your personal growth goals.

Similarly, setting clear milestones helps to maintain focus and motivation. Start by identifying short-term objectives, such as practicing meditation for ten minutes daily, and gradually build toward larger goals. Celebrate each achievement, no matter how small, as a testament to your dedication and growth.

How has my mindfulness practice already shaped my thoughts, emotions, and reactions, and where can I continue to grow?

Setting Future Mindfulness Goals

In today's fast-paced world, inner peace can seem elusive. However, formulating realistic and sustainable mindfulness objectives aligned with personal aspirations is a step forward in this journey. The SMART Goals Framework - Specific, Measurable, Achievable, Relevant, and Time-bound - provides an invaluable structure for your mindfulness progress. By applying this framework, you bring clarity to your mindfulness journey.

Specificity helps you focus on clear mindfulness objectives, such as dedicating ten minutes each morning to mindful meditation or observing your thoughts without judgment during moments of stress. Measurability ensures that you track your progress; for instance, by journaling your thoughts post-meditation, you actively measure your engagement and growth over time. Achievability is crucial, too, so set goals that are within reach yet challenging enough to inspire commitment. Set goals that are within reach yet challenging enough to inspire commitment, such as gradually increasing meditation duration rather than diving into hour-long sessions immediately. The relevance of these goals ties directly into aligning them with your core values, ensuring they resonate deeply and fulfill personal aspirations like enhancing emotional resilience or improving concentration. Lastly, time-bound elements encourage regular assessment of your progress, helping maintain momentum until mastery becomes a habit.

Aligning these goals with personal values enhances their resonance, making them more meaningful and integrated into your daily life. For example, if one of your values includes compassion, you might focus on mindfulness practices that foster empathy towards others and oneself. When mindfulness goals align with personal values, they become extensions of who you are, thus deepening their impact. Please reflect on what truly matters to you and tailor your mindfulness journey to align with those priorities. This connection sustains motivation and strengthens resilience in the face of challenges, knowing that your efforts are aligned with your true self. Without alignment, goals may feel foreign, creating disharmony rather than peace.

Incorporating flexibility into your approach allows your mindfulness practice to adapt to life's inevitable changes. At times, rigidity in goal setting can lead to feelings of failure or frustration when unexpected circumstances arise. However, viewing your mindfulness itinerary as a fluid plan allows room for adjustment, reducing overwhelm and staying balanced amidst shifts in your schedule or energy levels. It's about listening to your needs and responding with kindness, understanding that it's natural for goals to evolve alongside your life. This flexible mindset fosters a sustainable practice, nurturing growth without the pressure of rigid expectations.

Visualizing success involves imagining yourself achieving your mindfulness objectives, which enhances commitment and helps overcome self-doubt. Imagine closing your eyes and picturing a future where you've built a harmonious balance between work and relaxation, where stressors don't derail your peace. This imagery is a powerful motivator, embedding a sense of possibility and confidence. Success visualization encourages you to affirm that these achievements are attainable, reinforcing your dedication through perceived reality. By regularly engaging in this mental rehearsal, your mind starts to treat these scenarios as truth, paving the way for tangible outcomes.

While following these guidelines can be profoundly empowering, remember that this journey is unique to you. The principles of SMART goals and value alignment serve as a foundation, but personalizing them to fit your context is where fundamental transformation begins. Allow these frameworks to guide rather than dictate, leading you gently toward enduring mindfulness that aligns with your dreams and aspirations.

These structured approaches provide a roadmap, but cultivating inner peace requires patience and self-compassion. As you work toward your goals, give yourself grace for missteps, viewing them as learning opportunities rather than failures. Progress, not perfection, is the key. In doing so, you create a compassionate environment for yourself, ultimately fostering an inner landscape where peace and tranquility flourish naturally. With each step toward achieving your mindfulness objectives, visualize the end results and embrace the journey as a transformative experience that contributes to your growth.

Which mindfulness goals align most deeply with my core values, and how can I create a plan to integrate them into my daily life?

Strategies to Handle Setbacks

Understanding how to navigate setbacks is critical in pursuing inner peace. Often seen as failures, these moments can hinder progress and cause emotional turbulence. However, by reframing them as opportunities for growth, individuals can foster resilience. This shift empowers you to see challenges not as roadblocks but as pivotal experiences shaping your journey.

Mindfulness plays an essential role in this transformative process. Mindfulness techniques offer a reliable compass during setbacks, guiding us through turbulent emotions. Practicing mindfulness doesn't eliminate discomfort but helps anchor your thoughts and feelings, allowing you to observe them without judgment. For instance, when faced with disappointment, taking a moment to breathe deeply and ground ourselves helps to diminish automatic negative responses and opens the door to healthier processing of emotions. Regularly engaging in mindfulness exercises such as focused breathing or body scanning creates a mental buffer that cushions the impact of stressors and provides clarity.

Equally important is building a robust support system. Humans are inherently social beings, thriving on connections with others. Sharing experiences with trusted individuals can provide invaluable validation and accountability in challenging times. Friends, family, or support groups can act as sounding boards, offering different perspectives that help us reassess situations constructively. For example, discussing frustrations with a friend might reveal an overlooked aspect of a problem, sparking new ideas and solutions. Having someone to lean on can alleviate isolation, reduce stress, and promote healing.

Developing a resilience plan is another proactive approach to managing obstacles effectively. A well-thought-out plan acknowledges the inevitability of challenges and prepares strategies to address them head-on. This type of planning involves setting realistic expectations, identifying potential triggers that might lead to setbacks, and determining preemptive actions to counteract their effects. A practical part of this plan could be incorporating regular check-ins with oneself to assess emotional health or maintaining a journal to document thoughts and reflections. Such tools provide insight into recurring patterns and enable timely interventions before minor issues escalate.

Guidelines for these practices serve as helpful roadmaps during periods of uncertainty. One can start by scheduling short daily sessions dedicated to meditation or conscious breathing to integrate mindfulness techniques during setbacks. Consistency in practicing these methods enhances their effectiveness over time. It's helpful to create a quiet space free from distractions where these sessions can occur, reinforcing the habit and making it easier to turn to these practices when a setback arises.

A framework for developing a resilience plan might include setting aside specific times each week for reflection and adjustment. Review what's been working well and what hasn't, adjusting goals and strategies accordingly during these times. This iterative process ensures that the plan evolves alongside personal growth and changing circumstances, making it more adaptable and sustainable.

How can I reframe a recent setback in my mindfulness journey as an opportunity for growth and resilience?

Embracing Lifelong Mindfulness Journey

Embracing a lifelong commitment to mindfulness is a transformative journey for the mind and soul. Consistency in mindfulness practice is like watering a plant daily; the habit grows stronger with each session. This repetition solidifies mindfulness as a core part of one's routine and significantly enhances mental resilience. The benefits of maintaining this regular practice are profound, as practitioners often report improved cognitive functions and emotional stability over time (Seaver, 2023).

To ensure that mindfulness remains a dynamic and engaging part of life, it's essential to explore new practices regularly. As variety is vital to a balanced diet, integrating different mindfulness techniques can reinvigorate one's interest and prevent stagnation. Whether trying mindful walking, incorporating breathwork, or experimenting with body scan meditations, each new approach provides a fresh perspective and keeps the practice alive and enriching. This diversity promotes enthusiasm and keeps mindfulness from becoming a mundane task.

Continuing education is pivotal in deepening one's understanding of mindfulness principles. Attending workshops, reading new literature, or participating in online courses offers opportunities for expanding knowledge and keeping abreast of emerging research. This ongoing learning process fuels engagement, allowing individuals to update their techniques and apply them more effectively in various aspects of life. By staying informed, you can adapt your practices to suit your evolving needs, leading to sustained growth.

Living mindfully beyond structured practice is the ultimate goal of any mindfulness journey. It's about weaving mindfulness into the fabric of everyday life so it becomes a natural response rather than an isolated activity. Engaging in mindfulness during daily routines, like washing dishes or commuting, allows you to experience the present moment fully. It transforms ordinary activities into opportunities for mindfulness, fostering a deeper connection with oneself and the environment. Individuals can achieve a harmonious balance between their inner world and external experiences by cultivating this mindful awareness in all facets of life.

Some guidelines can be helpful for those new to integrating mindfulness into daily life. Start by identifying moments in your day when you can pause and breathe deeply, even if it's just for a minute. Gradually extend these pauses, allowing more time for reflection and presence. Use reminders, like phone alerts or sticky notes, to practice mindfulness consistently throughout the day until it becomes second nature. These small steps can significantly shift how one interacts with the world around them.

Mindfulness isn't solely an individual endeavor; it has communal aspects that can enhance its effects. Joining a group or community dedicated to mindfulness practice can provide support and shared experiences that enrich personal development. In these settings, people can share successes, learn from others, and receive feedback that broadens their perspective. Community involvement reinforces commitment and offers a sense of belonging, significantly enhancing the mindfulness journey.

Maintaining a journal can further support mindfulness integration into daily life. Writing down reflections about one's practice, emotions, and thoughts can reveal patterns and insights that might remain unnoticed. Journaling encourages self-awareness and personal accountability, allowing individuals to track their progress and recognize areas that need attention. This simple yet powerful tool can significantly deepen one's mindfulness practice, providing clarity and motivation to continue growing.

As mindfulness becomes integral to life, it naturally influences other areas, such as work, relationships, and personal well-being. Mindful individuals are often better equipped to handle stress, communicate more effectively, and form deeper connections with others. They cultivate an attitude of patience and empathy, which positively impacts social interactions. The ability to remain present, listen actively, and respond thoughtfully transforms relationships, creating a more compassionate and understanding environment.

Ultimately, embracing mindfulness as a lifelong commitment means continuously striving for balance and harmony within oneself and the world. It requires dedication, openness to change, and an eagerness to learn. Individuals can unlock lasting peace and fulfillment by approaching mindfulness with curiosity and compassion, guiding them toward a richer and more meaningful life.

What new mindfulness practices or techniques can I explore to keep my journey engaging and sustainable?

Closing Remarks

Our exploration shows that personal transformations through mindfulness hold powerful potential. You unlock a journey of self-discovery and growth by engaging in reflective journaling, setting attainable mindfulness goals, and developing resilience plans. These practices offer tools for embracing change, allowing for profound insights into your behaviors and emotions. Incorporating feedback from others enriches this understanding while celebrating milestones keeps motivation and progress visible. Mindfulness isn't just a practice but a way of living that encourages you to remain present and attuned to challenges and successes.

Navigating setbacks with mindfully cultivated resilience transforms perceived failures into learning opportunities, promoting stronger emotional regulation and self-awareness. As you integrate these strategies, remember that your journey is unique and personal. Embrace moments of reflection, flexibility in your goals, and the wisdom gained from past experiences. The consistent practice of mindfulness expands beyond structured sessions, weaving seamlessly into daily life. This lifelong commitment fosters an enduring sense of peace and fulfillment, bringing clarity to your mind and enriching every aspect of your existence. By cultivating mindfulness, you achieve a harmonious balance, unlocking a future filled with promise and tranquility.

What part of my daily routine could I begin integrating mindfulness into, allowing it to enrich my mind and overall well-being?

Here's what Megan learned from reading the chapter:

As Megan reached the final chapter, she felt a sense of accomplishment and motivation to embrace the lifelong journey of mindfulness fully. The idea of reflecting on personal transformations struck her as particularly important. She realized how much she had grown since starting her mindfulness practice, especially in managing stress and being more present with herself and others. This chapter encouraged her to journal consistently, something she had always wanted to do but never prioritized. Megan liked the idea of using a journal to track her progress, identify patterns in her emotions, and celebrate milestones, which would help her stay focused and motivated.

Setting future mindfulness goals using the SMART framework was another critical takeaway for Megan. She appreciated this method's structure, especially since it allowed her to create realistic goals that align with her core values, such as reducing anxiety and fostering empathy in her relationships. She planned to start with small, achievable goals, like meditating for ten minutes each morning and practicing mindful breathing during her commute. These goals would allow her to maintain flexibility while working towards a more profound inner peace.

The section on handling setbacks resonated with her deeply. Megan recognized that setbacks were a part of any personal growth journey, and this chapter reframed them as opportunities for learning rather than failures. She was inspired to develop her resilience plan to help her manage stress and emotional triggers more effectively. Having a plan in place gave her the confidence to navigate challenges without being derailed.

The concept of lifelong mindfulness also sparked Megan's excitement. She felt ready to explore new mindfulness practices to keep her journey engaging and sustainable. She wanted to experiment with mindful walking and body scan meditations, as they offered new ways to connect with her body and emotions. Megan also considered joining a local mindfulness group to stay motivated and share experiences with others on a similar path.

Overall, this chapter reinforced that mindfulness is not a one-time solution but an ongoing practice. Megan felt empowered to continue growing, embracing both the triumphs and challenges along the way. She saw mindfulness as a tool for managing stress and a way of life that would bring balance, clarity, and fulfillment. Moving forward, she planned to integrate mindfulness into her daily routine, from work to personal relationships, ensuring that this practice would enrich every part of her life.

Amelie Brooks

How This Book Helped Megan on Her Journey to Get Better

When Megan first picked up this book, she wasn't expecting it to solve all her problems overnight. Instead, she was searching for guidance that could help her navigate the stress and overwhelm she often felt. She found a set of practical tools that didn't promise quick fixes but offered a path toward sustainable, long-term improvements.

From the very beginning, Megan realized that mindfulness wasn't something that could instantly change her life. The book taught her that genuine growth comes from small, consistent efforts and provided her with a framework to make those efforts a regular part of her routine. One of the biggest lessons she took away was the importance of patience—both with herself and the process. She learned that progress takes time and that setbacks didn't mean failure but were simply part of her journey.

The practice of mindful journaling was one of the first tools Megan embraced. Although initially felt strange, it gradually became a way for her to reconnect with her thoughts and emotions. By regularly writing down her experiences, she started to notice patterns in her reactions to stress and anxiety. With that awareness, she began making subtle shifts in approaching these challenges. Journaling didn't eliminate the stress from her life, but it helped her understand it better, allowing her to respond more clearly.

Another key takeaway for Megan was the importance of setting realistic goals. Before reading the book, she often felt pressure to achieve significant, sweeping changes. But the book helped her see that starting small - like practicing mindfulness for just five minutes a day - was far more sustainable. As she gradually increased her time on mindfulness practices, Megan found that these small steps had a lasting impact. She didn't feel overwhelmed; over time, these moments of mindfulness became a natural part of her day.

One of the most significant changes Megan experienced was her ability to deal with setbacks. Before, missing a day of mindfulness practice or feeling overwhelmed might have derailed her progress. But the book helped her reframe those moments, teaching her to view setbacks not as failures but as opportunities to learn and grow. This mindset shift allowed Megan to continue her practice without the guilt or frustration often accompanying such moments.

Megan also began to incorporate mindfulness into her daily activities more naturally. Instead of seeing mindfulness as something that had to be scheduled or done in a quiet room, she learned to bring mindfulness into everyday moments—whether walking, cooking, or having a conversation. This approach helped her stay grounded throughout the day, making mindfulness feel more fluid and integrated into her life.

The book didn't solve all of Megan's problems, but it gave her the tools to navigate them with more resilience and awareness. Over time, these mindfulness techniques became part of her toolkit for managing stress and anxiety, and they helped her build a stronger connection with herself. While Megan knew she was still on her journey, she felt more equipped to handle life's challenges and more at peace with the ups and downs that came her way.

Amelie Brooks

In reflection, this book acted as a gentle guide for Megan, not by offering instant solutions but by helping her create habits that would improve her well-being over time. It didn't promise a perfect life, but it showed her how to find moments of clarity and calm amid life's chaos, which made all the difference.

Conclusion

As you reach the end of our journey together, let's take a moment to reflect on the transformative lessons you've uncovered. You began by acknowledging the relentless loops of overthinking that can ensnare your mind, leaving you feeling paralyzed and overwhelmed. This recognition was crucial. It marked the first step in reclaiming control over your thoughts and emotions. By identifying what triggers our spirals of anxious thinking, we have empowered ourselves to make conscious decisions instead of being ruled by automatic reactions.

Throughout this book, you've delved into mindfulness practices, uncovering their profound impact on your mental clarity and emotional well-being. Mindfulness teaches you to live in the present moment, to observe your thoughts without judgment, and to create space between stimulus and response. In doing so, you break free from the chains of overthinking and embrace a more centered, peaceful existence. Each chapter has equipped you with tools and insights to cultivate mindfulness, empowering you to transform your relationship with your mind.

In today's fast-paced world, where demands and distractions abound, the relevance of mindfulness cannot be overstated. It's not an elusive or esoteric practice reserved for the spiritually inclined; it's a practical, accessible approach anyone can incorporate into daily life. From savoring your morning coffee to consciously breathing during a hectic workday, mindfulness offers a sanctuary from chaos, a way to tune into the present and anchor yourself amidst life's storms.

Amelie Brooks

Mindfulness is powerful, but it requires commitment and practice like any worthwhile endeavor. As you've learned throughout these chapters, the benefits of mindfulness are manifold: reduced anxiety, increased emotional intelligence, improved focus, and enhanced overall quality of life. However, the journey toward establishing a mindful practice can be complicated. There will be times when it feels challenging—when the noise of life drowns out your intentions. Remember, this is normal, and every mindful breath you take is progress.

Imagine your future self - a year from now - reflecting on your embarked journey. Think about the skills you've honed, the moments of clarity illuminating your path, and the peace that has gradually seeped into your everyday life. Envision setting personal goals that align with your lifestyle and values, allowing mindfulness to blossom naturally within your unique circumstances. Your intentions today are stepping stones paving the way for tomorrow's mindfulness.

As you conclude, I urge you not just to close the book and move on but to integrate the wisdom shared here into the fabric of your life. Mindfulness is a lifelong companion that can be called upon whenever needed, whether encountering a stressful situation or simply seeking greater joy in mundane moments. Share your journey with others - friends, family, or online communities - to inspire and support one another as you navigate life's challenges together. By sharing, you amplify the light mindfulness brings, spreading its positive ripple effects far beyond yourself.

Just to remind you, this book is just the starting point. The real adventure begins now as you apply what you've learned and witness mindfulness's gradual yet profound impact on your life. Embrace each opportunity to bring presence into your day, knowing that mindfulness can transform ordinary experiences into extraordinary ones. Whether finding solace in quiet reflection or practicing mindfulness on the go, allow yourself the flexibility to experiment and see what resonates most with you.

Remember, mindfulness is not about achieving a state of perpetual bliss or eliminating all negative emotions. It's about creating a dynamic resilience, an ability to navigate joy and sorrow with grace and awareness. As you continue to grow in your practice, you'll likely find that your understanding deepens and evolves. Be patient with yourself and trust the process, recognizing that every moment spent in mindfulness is a gift you give yourself.

Now is the moment to fully embark on this mindful journey. Take the courageous step to incorporate the practices and exercises in this book into your daily routine. Allow them to guide you toward inner peace and a deeper understanding of yourself. And in doing so, you'll illuminate a path for yourself and those who walk alongside you in this life. Together, let's nurture a world where mindfulness becomes a natural part of our lives, enriching interactions, enhancing relationships, and fostering a collective consciousness grounded in compassion and presence.

Thank you for joining me on this exploration of the mind and spirit. May you continue to discover mindfulness's beauty and tranquility, and may you share this gift with the world around you. As you part ways on this journey, know that you carry

Amelie Brooks

within you the power to transform your own life and those you touch. Here's to a future filled with mindful moments, enriched connections, and a life in harmony with the present.

Reader Acknowledgement

Thank you for taking the time to read this book. I hope the insights and strategies shared here have been meaningful to you and brought some peace and clarity into your life. Your journey through these pages means a lot, and it's my sincere wish that you found value in the tips and practices we explored together.

If you enjoyed the book and found it helpful, I would truly appreciate it if you could take a moment to leave a review. Your feedback not only helps other readers discover the book but also encourages me to continue creating content that supports personal growth and well-being. Thank you once again for allowing this book to be a part of your journey.

References

Blocked. (2024). Fndhealth.com. https://www.fndhealth.com/post/the-mind-body-connection-how-overthinking-and-mental-stress-impact-physical-health

Brennan, D. (2020, December 3). *Burnout: Symptoms and Signs.* WebMD; WebMD. https://www.webmd.com/mental-health/burnout-symptoms-signs

Is Decision Overload Affecting Your Mental Health? (2023). Psychology Today. https://www.psychologytoday.com/intl/blog/high-octane-women/202306/is-decision-overload-affecting-your-mental-health

NHS. (2021). *Symptoms - Generalised anxiety disorder in adults.* Nhs.uk. https://www.nhs.uk/mental-health/conditions/generalised-anxiety-disorder/symptoms/

OITE Blog - NIH office of Intramural Research | Overthinking and Underperforming. (2024). Nih.gov. https://oitecareersblog.od.nih.gov/2023/06/12/overthinking-and-underperforming

Overthinking Disorder: Is It a Mental Illness? (2022, May 16). Cleveland Clinic. https://health.clevelandclinic.org/is-overthinking-a-mental-illness

Renoir, T., Hasebe, K., & Gray, L. (2013, December 18). *Mind and body: how the health of the body impacts on neuropsychiatry.* Frontiers in Pharmacology. https://doi.org/10.3389/fphar.2013.00158

Sperber, S. (2023). *Overthinking: Definition, Causes, & How to Stop Overthinking*. The Berkeley Well-Being Institute. https://www.berkeleywellbeing.com/overthinking.htm

Goldman Schuyler, K., Watson, L. W., & King, E. (2021, December). *How Generative Mindfulness Can Contribute to Inclusive Workplaces*. Humanistic Management Journal. https://doi.org/10.1007/s41463-021-00120-2

Hofmann, S. G., & Gómez, A. F. (2017). *Mindfulness-Based Interventions for Anxiety and Depression*. Psychiatric Clinics of North America. https://doi.org/10.1016/j.psc.2017.08.008

Keng, S. L., Smoski, M. J., & Robins, C. J. (2011, May 13). *Effects of Mindfulness on Psychological health: a Review of Empirical Studies*. Clinical Psychology Review. https://doi.org/10.1016/j.cpr.2011.04.006

Madeson, M. (2022, October 27). *Mindfulness in counseling: 8 best techniques & interventions*. PositivePsychology.com. https://positivepsychology.com/mindfulness-in-counseling/

Selva, J. (2017, March 13). *History of Mindfulness: from East to West and Religion to Science*. PositivePsychology.com. https://positivepsychology.com/history-of-mindfulness/

TikTok - Make Your Day. (2024). Tiktok.com. https://www.tiktok.com/@dzigbordikwakudosoo/video/7329561210595167489

Brennan, D. (2021). *What to Know About 4-7-8 Breathing*. WebMD. https://www.webmd.com/balance/what-to-know-4-7-8-breathing

Collins-O, C. (2024, January 31). *Mastering Personal Development in the Digital Age: Understanding the Power of Habit and Mindfulness.* Medium. https://medium.com/@c.collins.c624/mastering-personal-development-in-the-digital-age-understanding-the-power-of-habit-and-mindfulness-cd3937350966

Department of Health & Human Services. (2015). *Breathing to reduce stress.* Www.betterhealth.vic.gov.au. https://www.betterhealth.vic.gov.au/health/healthyliving/breathing-to-reduce-stress

Fletcher, J. (2019, February 12). *4-7-8 breathing: How it works, benefits, and uses.* Medical News Today. https://www.medicalnewstoday.com/articles/324417

Harvard Health Publishing. (2020, July 6). *Relaxation techniques: Breath control helps quell errant stress response - Harvard Health.* Harvard Health; Harvard Health. https://www.health.harvard.edu/mind-and-mood/relaxation-techniques-breath-control-helps-quell-errant-stress-response

Habit. (2024). *Habit Formation: Mindful Awareness: Cultivating Mindful Awareness to Enhance Habit Formation - FasterCapital.* FasterCapital. https://fastercapital.com/content/Habit-Formation--Mindful-Awareness--Cultivating-Mindful-Awareness-to-Enhance-Habit-Formation.html

Telloian, C. (2021, October 4). *All About Mindful Breathing.* Psych Central; Psych Central. https://psychcentral.com/health/mindful-breathing

A Complete Guide To Journaling For Spiritual Growth And Self-Development. (2021, February 4). MindThatEgo. https://www.mindthatego.com/journaling-for-spiritual-growth/

Bégin, C., Berthod, J., Martinez, L. Z., & Truchon, M. (2022, September 6). *Use of Mobile Apps and Online Programs of Mindfulness and Self-Compassion Training in Workers: A Scoping Review.* Journal of Technology in Behavioral Science. https://doi.org/10.1007/s41347-022-00267-1

Creating Your Perfect Meditation Space | The Balance App. (n.d.). Balanceapp.com. https://balanceapp.com/blog/crafting-your-ideal-meditation-space

Flynn, L. (2024, June 8). *Creating a Meditation Space at Home | 9 Tips.* Lavender & Laurel; Lavender & Laurel. https://www.lavenderandlaurelhome.com/post/creating-a-meditation-space-at-home-9-tips

Morales-Brown, P. (2023, May 24). *7 types of meditation: What type is best for you?* Www.medicalnewstoday.com. https://www.medicalnewstoday.com/articles/320392

Schwartz, K., Fabienne Marie Ganster, & Tran, U. S. (2023, August 4). *Mindfulness-Based Mobile Apps and Their Impact on Well-Being in Nonclinical Populations: Systematic Review of Randomized Controlled Trials.* Journal of Medical Internet Research; JMIR Publications. https://doi.org/10.2196/44638

happiness.com. (2021, March 10). Happiness.com. https://www.happiness.com/magazine/inspiration-spirituality/introduction-meditation-styles/

rootlessadventurecompany@gmail.com. (2023, August 30). *Exploring the Benefits of Daily Journaling and Meditation - Rootless Adventure Co.* Rootless Adventure Co -. https://rootlessadventurecompany.com/2023/08/30/exploring-the-benefits-of-daily-journaling-and-meditation/

Bay. (2024, September 15). *Top Cognitive Behavioral Therapy Exercises for Better Mental Health.* Bay Area CBT Center. https://bayareacbtcenter.com/cognitive-behavioral-therapy-exercises/

Caporuscio, J. (2020, March 31). *Grounding techniques for anxiety, PTSD, and trauma.* Www.medicalnewstoday.com. https://www.medicalnewstoday.com/articles/grounding-techniques

Doll, K. (2019, March 23). *23 Resilience Building Tools and Exercises (+ Mental Toughness Test).* PositivePsychology.com. https://positivepsychology.com/resilience-activities-exercises/

Lane, R. D., & Smith, R. (2021, August 19). *Levels of Emotional Awareness: Theory and Measurement of a Socio-Emotional Skill.* Journal of Intelligence. https://doi.org/10.3390/jintelligence9030042

National Institutes of Health. (2022). *Emotional wellness toolkit.* National Institutes of Health (NIH). https://www.nih.gov/health-information/emotional-wellness-toolkit

Practicing Pausing (STOP) - Wisdom & Wellbeing Program. (n.d.). www.medicalcenter.virginia.edu. https://www.medicalcenter.virginia.edu/wwp/positive-practices-to-enhance-resilience-and-improve-interpersonal-communication-individual-techniques-1/self-regulation/practicing-pausing-stop/

Treatment, M. (2023, December 1). *The Benefits of Using Mindfulness-Based Practices for Emotional Regulation.* Mississippi Drug and Alcohol Treatment Center. https://mississippidatc.com/the-benefits-of-using-mindfulness-based-practices-for-emotional-regulation/

Vine, V., Boyd, R. L., & Pennebaker, J. W. (2020, September 10). *Natural emotion vocabularies as windows on distress and well-being.* Nature Communications. https://doi.org/10.1038/s41467-020-18349-0

Gibson, J. (2019, September 13). *Mindfulness, Interoception, and the Body: A Contemporary Perspective.* Frontiers in Psychology. https://doi.org/10.3389/fpsyg.2019.02012

Mindfulness and breathing techniques for exam stress. (n.d.). Birmingham City University. https://www.bcu.ac.uk/exams-and-revision/wellbeing/mindfulness-and-breathing-techniques

Mayo Clinic. (2020, September 15). *Mindfulness exercises.* Mayo Clinic. https://www.mayoclinic.org/healthy-lifestyle/consumer-health/in-depth/mindfulness-exercises/art-20046356

Raypole, C. (2020, March 26). *Body Scan Meditation: Benefits and How to Do It.* Healthline. https://www.healthline.com/health/body-scan-meditation

Scott, E. (2024, February 12). *What is body scan meditation?* Verywell Mind. https://www.verywellmind.com/body-scan-meditation-why-and-how-3144782

The many benefits of mindful body scan meditations. (2024, March 21). Mindfulness for Better Living. https://www.canr.msu.edu/news/the-many-benefits-of-mindful-body-scan-meditations

Art. (2023, December 8). *Niche Pilates Studio*. Niche Pilates Studio. https://www.nichefitstudio.com/education-blog/the-art-of-mindful-movement-unveiling-the-power-of-breath

Dance as a Tool for Emotional Expression and Self-Management. (n.d.). Www.classcardapp.com. https://www.classcardapp.com/blog/dance-as-a-tool-for-emotional-expression-and-self-management

Díaz-Silveira, C., Alcover, C.-M., Burgos, F., Marcos, A., & Santed, M. A. (2020, April 20). *Mindfulness versus Physical Exercise: Effects of Two Recovery Strategies on Mental Health, Stress and Immunoglobulin A during Lunch Breaks. A Randomized Controlled Trial*. International Journal of Environmental Research and Public Health. https://doi.org/10.3390/ijerph17082839

Department of Health & Human Services. (2015). *Breathing to reduce stress*. Www.betterhealth.vic.gov.au. https://www.betterhealth.vic.gov.au/health/healthyliving/breathing-to-reduce-stress

Payton Solk, Auster-Gussman, L., Torre, E., Welch, W. A., Murphy, K., Starikovsky, J., Reading, J. M., Victorson, D., & Phillips, S. M. (2023, November 10). *Effects of mindful physical activity on perceived exercise exertion and other physiological and psychological responses: results from a within-subjects, counter-balanced study*. Frontiers in

Psychology; Frontiers Media. https://doi.org/10.3389/fpsyg.2023.1285315

Sandstrom, M. (2024, January 18). *Mindful Movements: Integrating Wellness into Your Daily Routine - Molly My*. Molly My. https://mollymy.com/wellness/mindful-movements-integrating-wellness-into-your-daily-routine/

Zhang, X., & Wei, Y. (2024, August 1). *The Role of Dance Movement Therapy in Enhancing Emotional Regulation: A Literature Review*. Heliyon; Elsevier BV. https://doi.org/10.1016/j.heliyon.2024.e35733

tylorBennett. (2024, July 17). *Integrating Mindfulness Practices into Daily Life - Eastside Ideal Health*. Eastside Ideal Health. https://www.eastsideidealhealth.com/integrating-mindfulness-practices-into-daily-life/

Hong, M. N. (2023, November 30). *Transforming Self-Care: How I Use ChatGPT for Reflective Journaling*. Medium. https://mandynicolehong.medium.com/transforming-self-care-how-i-use-chatgpt-for-reflective-journaling-bce5cdaf8c2a

How to Stay Motivated and Consistent During Your Meditation Practice [Episode #818] | Solluna by Kimberly Snyder. (2023, September 7). Solluna, by Kimberly Snyder. https://mysolluna.com/blog/how-to-stay-motivated-and-consistent-during-your-meditation-practice-episode-818/

Keng, S. L., Smoski, M. J., & Robins, C. J. (2011, May 13). *Effects of Mindfulness on Psychological health: a Review of Empirical Studies*. Clinical Psychology Review. https://doi.org/10.1016/j.cpr.2011.04.006

Moving From Anxiety to Excitement – Toby Ouvry Meditation. (2015). Tobyouvry.com. https://tobyouvry.com/2015/06/moving-from-anxiety-to-excitement/

Matthias, C., Bu, C., Cohen, M., Jones, M. V., & Hearn, J. H. (2024, August 2). *The role of mindfulness in stress, productivity and wellbeing of foundation year doctors: a mixed-methods feasibility study of the mindful resilience and effectiveness training programme.* BMC Medical Education; BioMed Central. https://doi.org/10.1186/s12909-024-05810-7

Rosebud - AI Journal for Personal Growth. (n.d.). Www.rosebud.app. https://www.rosebud.app/

Schuman-Olivier, Z., Trombka, M., Lovas, D. A., Brewer, J. A., Vago, D. R., Gawande, R., Dunne, J. P., Lazar, S. W., Loucks, E. B., & Fulwiler, C. (2020). *Mindfulness and behavior change.* Harvard Review of Psychiatry. https://doi.org/10.1097/HRP.0000000000000277

Sawyer, H. (2023, February 13). *Mindfulness: Strategies to implement targeted self-care.* Journal of Interprofessional Education & Practice. https://doi.org/10.1016/j.xjep.2023.100614

Carter, A., Tobias, J. M., & Kate Lauren Spiegelhalter. (2016, November 15). *Mindfulness in organisations Case studies of organisational practice.* ResearchGate; unknown. https://www.researchgate.net/publication/310587213_Mindfulness_in_organisations_Case_studies_of_organisational_practice

Craig, H. (2019, June 19). *Mindfulness at Work: Using Mindful Leadership in the Workplace (Incl. Tips)*. PositivePsychology.com. https://positivepsychology.com/mindfulness-at-work/

DBT Skills Interpersonal Effectiveness | Rethinking Residency. (2023, February 17). Rethinking Residency. https://rethinkingresidency.com/wellness-resources/dbt-skills/dbt-skills-for-increasing-interpersonal-effectiveness/

Goyal, M., Singh, S., Sibinga, E. M. S., Gould, N. F., Rowland-Seymour, A., Sharma, R., Berger, Z., Sleicher, D., Maron, D. D., Shihab, H. M., Ranasinghe, P. D., Linn, S., Saha, S., Bass, E. B., & Haythornthwaite, J. A. (2014, March 1). *Meditation Programs for Psychological Stress and Well-being*. JAMA Internal Medicine. https://doi.org/10.1001/jamainternmed.2013.13018

Kriakous, S. A., Elliott, K. A., Lamers, C., & Owen, R. (2020, September 24). *The Effectiveness of mindfulness-based Stress Reduction on the Psychological Functioning of Healthcare professionals: a Systematic Review*. Mindfulness. https://doi.org/10.1007/s12671-020-01500-9

Leaf, O. (2024, May 31). *Olive Leaf Therapy*. Olive Leaf Therapy. https://www.oliveleaftherapy.com/blog/enhancing-interpersonal-communication-skills

McCutcheon, S. (2022, June 2). *10 Mindblowing Benefits of Mindfulness at Work*. Champion Health. https://championhealth.co.uk/insights/benefits-mindfulness-at-work/

7 Ways to Build Resilience in Times of Career Uncertainty - Employment Enterprises. (2024, September 25). Employment Enterprises. https://eeihr.com/blog/employment-expert/7-ways-to-build-resilience-in-times-of-career-uncertainty/

Hölzel, B. K., Carmody, J., Vangel, M., Congleton, C., Yerramsetti, S. M., Gard, T., & Lazar, S. W. (2011, January 30). *Mindfulness practice leads to increases in regional brain gray matter density.* Psychiatry Research: Neuroimaging. https://doi.org/10.1016/j.pscychresns.2010.08.006

Handcrafted Marketing Solutions. (2024, January 30). *Building Resilience: Therapy Techniques for Overcoming Life's Challenges.* Hearttoheartcounsel. https://www.h2hsarasota.com/post/building-resilience-therapy-techniques-for-overcoming-life-s-challenges

Journaling to increase self-awareness. (n.d.). Prosper. https://prosper.liverpool.ac.uk/postdoc-resources/reflect/journaling-to-increase-self-awareness/

Seaver, M. (2023, August 9). *What Mindfulness Does to Your Brain: The Science of Neuroplasticity.* Real Simple. https://www.realsimple.com/health/mind-mood/mindfulness-improves-brain-health-neuroplasticity

Thompson, N. (2013, March 15). *Smart Goals and the Law of Attraction - Vibe Shifting.* Vibe Shifting. https://www.vibeshifting.com/smart-goals-and-law-of-attraction/

Wright, K. W. (2023, June 21). *Emotional Journaling: How to Use Journaling to Process Emotions.* Day One | Your Journal for Life. https://dayoneapp.com/blog/emotional-journaling/

psicosmart.pro. (2024). *Integrating Mindfulness Practices into the SMART Goal Setting Process.* Psicosmart.pro. https://psicosmart.pro/en/blogs/blog-integrating-mindfulness-practices-into-the-smart-goal-setting-process-190492

Rosenberger, Amelia. "Take Deep Breaths." ITA Journal, vol. 48, no. 1, 2020, pp. 18-20.

Morrell, Linda. "A Handbook of Interventions and Supportive Counselling Methods for Facilitating a "Good" Death." 2008, https://core.ac.uk/download/185287093.pdf.

"Take your breathing to an even deeper level". https://www.reclaimedbeing.com/post/design-a-stunning-blog

Reaping the Benefits of Relaxation | Designing Brighter Tomorrows. https://designingbrightertomorrows.org/health/reaping-the-benefits-of-relaxation/

Harnessing the Healing Power of Breath: A Journey to Pain Relief. https://www.miakhalilcoaching.com/post/harnessing-the-healing-power-of-breath-a-journey-to-pain-relief

Finding Joy Meditation 08 - Guided Meditation VR. https://guidedmeditationvr.com/finding-joy-8/

The Dreaded Golf Shank: Causes, Prevention, and Outlook – Whole in One. https://wholeinonebar.com/blogs/articles/the-dreaded-golf-shank-causes-prevention-and-outlook

Digital Distractions and Emotional Intelligence Strategies for Staying Focused – Dr. Anju Chawla. https://www.anjuchawla.com/digital-distractions-and-emotional-intelligence-strategies-for-staying-focused/